How to See a Play

Richard Francis Burton

Addendum by Sasha Newborn

Mudborn Press

How to See a Play © 2015 Mudborn Press
ISBN 978-0-930012-70-0

MUDBORN PRESS
an imprint of Bandanna Books
(www.bandannabooks.com)
is devoted to
minor classics and bilingual texts
from many traditions,
stories that tell us
where we came from,
and help us to
where we are going.

RELATED TITLES:
The Art of Writing, Robert Louis Stevenson
How to Tell a Story, Mark Twain
How to Write..., Edgar Allan Poe
Write It Right, Ambrose Bierce
and Shakespeare plays.

See catalog at back of book

Contents

Preface	5
Chapter 1 The Play, a Form of Storytelling	7
Chapter 2 The Play, a Cultural Opportunity	17
Chapter 3 Up to Shakespeare	28
Chapter 4 Growth to the Nineteenth Century	40
Chapter 5 The Modern School	59
Chapter 6 The Play as Theme and Personal View	62
Chapter 7 Method and Structure	71
Chapter 8 Development	80
Chapter 9 Climax	89
Chapter 10 Ending the Play	100
Chapter 11 The Social Significance of the Play	110
Addendum	123
Catalog	126

Now here are twenty critics ... and yet every one is a critic after his own way; that is, *such a play is best because I like it*. A very familiar argument, methinks, to prove the excellence of a play, and to which an author would be very unwilling to appeal for his success.

—from Farquhar's
A Discourse Upon Comedy

Preface

This book is aimed squarely at the theater-goer. It hopes to offer a concise general treatment upon the use of the theater, so that the person in the seat may get the most for his money; may choose his entertainment wisely, avoid that which is not worth while, and appreciate the values artistic and intellectual of what he is seeing and hearing.

This purpose should be borne in mind, in reading the book, for while I trust the critic and the playwright may find the discussion not without interest and sane in principle, the desire is primarily to put into the hands of the many who attend the playhouse a manual that will prove helpful and, so far as it goes, be an influence toward creating in this country that body of alert theater auditors without which good drama will not flourish. The obligation of the theater-goer to insist on sound plays is one too long overlooked; and just in so far as he does insist in ever-growing numbers upon drama that has technical skill, literary quality and interpretive insight into life, will that better theater come which must be the hope of all who realize the great social and educative powers of the playhouse. The words of that veteran actor-manager and playwright of the past, Colley Cibber, are apposite here: "It is not to the actor therefore, but to the vitiated and low taste of the spectator, that the corruptions of the stage (of what kind soever) have been owing. If the public, by whom they must live, had spirit enough to discountenance and declare against all the trash and fopperies they have been so frequently fond of, both the actors and the authors, to the best of their power, must naturally have served their daily table with sound and wholesome diet." And again he remarks: "For as their hearers are, so will actors be; worse or better, as the false or true taste applauds or discommends them. Hence only can our theaters improve, or must degenerate." Not for a moment is it implied that this book, or any book of the kind, can make playwrights. Playwrights as well as actors are born, not made—at least, in the sense that seeing life dramatically and having a feeling for situation and climax is a gift and nothing else. The wise Cibber may be heard also upon this. "To excel in either art," he declares, "is a self-born happiness, which something more than good sense must be mother of." But this may be granted, while it is maintained stoutly that there remains to the dramatist a technique to be acquired, and that practice therein and reflection upon it makes perfect. The would-be playwright can learn his trade, even as another, and must, to succeed. And the spectator (our main point of attack, as was said), the necessary coadjutor with player and playwright in theater success, can also become an adept in his part of this cooperative result. This book is written to assist him in such cooperation.

Chapter 1

The Play, a Form of Storytelling

The play is a form of story telling, among several such forms: the short story, or tale; the novel; and in verse, the epic and that abbreviated version of it called the ballad. All of them, each in its own fashion, is trying to do pretty much the same thing, to tell a story. And by story, as the word is used in this book, it will be well to say that I mean such a manipulation of human happenings as to give a sense of unity and growth to a definite end. A story implies a connection of characters and events so as to suggest a rounding out and completion, which, looked back upon, shall satisfy man's desire to discover some meaning and significance in what is called Life. A child begging at the mother's knee for "the end of the story," before bedtime, really represents the race; the instinct behind the request is a sound one. A story, then, has a beginning, middle and end, and in the right hands is seen to have proportion, organic cohesion and development. Its parts dovetail, and what at first appeared to lack direction and connective significance finally is seen to possess that wholeness which makes it a work of art. A story, therefore, is not a chance medley of incidents and characters; but an artistic texture so woven as to quicken our feeling that a universe which often seems disordered and chance-wise is in reality ordered and pre-arranged. Art in its story-making does this service for life, even if life does not do it for us. And herein lies one of the differences between art and life; art, as it were, going life one better in this rearrangement of material.

Of the various ways referred to of telling a story, the play has its distinctive method and characteristics, to separate it from the others. The story is told on a stage, through the impersonation of character by human beings; in word and action, assisted by scenery, the story is unfolded. The drama (a term used doubly to mean plays in general or some particular play) is distinguished from the other forms mentioned in substituting dialogue and direct visualized action for the indirect narration of fiction.

A play when printed differs also in certain ways; the persons of the play are named apart from the text; the speakers are indicated by writing their names before the speeches; the action is indicated in parentheses, the name business being given to this supplementary information, the same term that is used on the stage for all that lies outside dialogue and scenery. And the whole play, as a rule, is sub-divided into acts and often, especially in earlier drama, into scenes, lesser divisions within the acts; these divisions being used for purposes of better handling of the plot and exigencies of scene shifting, as well as for agreeable breathing spaces for the audience. The word scene, it may be added here, is used in English-speaking lands to indicate a change of scene, whereas in foreign drama it merely refers to the exit or entrance of a character, so that a different number of persons is on the stage.

But there are, of course, deeper, more organic qualities than these external attributes of a play. The stern limits of time in the representation of the stage story—little more than two hours, "the two hours traffic of the stage" mentioned by Shakespeare—necessitates telling the story with emphasis upon its salient points; only the high lights of character and event can be advantageously shown within such limits. Hence the dramatic story, as the adjective has come to show, indicates a story presenting in a terse and telling fashion only the most important and exciting things. To be dramatic is thus to be striking, to produce effects by omission, compression, stress and crescendo. To be sure, recent modern plays can be named in plenty which seem to violate this principle; but they do so at their peril, and in the history of drama nothing is plainer than that the essence of good play-making lies in the power to seize the significant moments of the stage story and so present them as to grip the interest and hold it with increasing tension up to a culminating moment called the climax.

Certain advantages and certain limitations follow from these characteristics of a play. For one thing, the drama is able to focus on the really interesting, exciting, enthralling moments of human doings, where a novel, for example, which has so much more leisure to accomplish its purpose to give a picture of life, can afford to take its time and becomes slower, and often, as a result, comparatively prolix and indirect. This may not be advisable in a piece of fiction, but it is often found, and masterpieces both of the past and present illustrate the possibility; the work of a Richardson, a Henry James, a Bennett. But for a play this would be simply suicide; for the drama must be more direct, condensed and rapid. And just in proportion as a novel adopts the method of the play do we call it dramatic and does it win a general audience; the story of a Stevenson or a Kipling.

Again, having in mind the advantages of the play, the stage story is both heard and seen, and important results issue from this fact. The play-story is actually seen instead of seen by the eye of the imagination through the appeal of the printed page; or indirectly again, if one hears a narrative recited. And this actual seeing on the stage brings conviction, since "seeing is believing," by the old saw. Scenery, too, necessitates a certain truthfulness in the reproducing of life by word and act and scene, because the spectator, who is able to judge it all by the test of life, will more readily compare the mimic representation with the actuality than if he were reading the words of a character in a book, or being told, narrative fashion, of the character's action. In this way the stage story seems nearer life.

Moreover, the seeing is fortified by hearing; the spectator is also the auditor. And here is another test of reality. If the intonation or accent or tone of voice of the actor is not life-like and in consonance with the character portrayed, the audience will instantly be quicker to detect it and to criticize than if the same character were shown in fiction; seeing, the spectator insists that dress and carriage, and scenery, which furnishes a congruous background, shall be plausible; and hearing, the auditor insists upon the speech being true to type.

The play has an immense superiority also over all printed literature in that, making its appeal directly through eye and ear, it is not literary at all; I mean, the story in this form can be understood and enjoyed by countless who read but little or even cannot read. Literature, in the conventional sense, may be a closed book to innumerable theater-goers who nevertheless can witness a drama and react to its exhibition of life. The word, which in printed letters is so all-important, on the stage becomes secondary to action and scene, for the story can be, and sometimes is, enacted in pantomime, without a single word being spoken. In essence, therefore, a play may be called unliterary, and thus it makes a wider, more democratic appeal than anything in print can. Yet, by an interesting paradox, when the words of the play are written by masters like Calderón, Shakespeare, Molière or Ibsen, the drama becomes the chief literary glory of Spain, England, France and Norway. For in the final reckoning only the language that is fit and fine preserves the drama of the world in books and classifies it with creative literature. Thus the play can be all things to all men; at once unliterary in its appeal, and yet, in the finest examples, an important contribution to letters.

A peculiar advantage of the play over the other story-telling forms is found in the fact that while one reads the printed story, short or long, the epic or ballad, by oneself in the quiet enjoyment of the library, one witnesses the drama in company with many other human beings—unless the play be a dire failure and the house empty. And this association, though it may remove some of the more refined and aristocratic experiences of the reader, has a definite effect upon individual pleasure in the way of enrichment, and even reacts upon the play itself to shape its nature. A curious sort of sympathy is set up throughout an audience as it receives the skillful story of the playwright; common or crowd emotions are aroused, personal variations are submerged in a general associative feeling and the individual does not so much laugh, cry and wonder by himself as do these things sympathetically in conjunction with others. He becomes a simpler, less complex person whose emotions dominate the analytic processes of the individual brain. He is a more plastic receptive creature than he would be alone. Any one can test this for himself by asking if he would have laughed so uproariously at a certain humorous speech had it been offered him detached from the time and place. The chances are that, by and in itself, it might not seem funny at all. And the readiness with which he fell into cordial conversation with the stranger in the next seat is also a hint as to his magnetized mood when thus subjected to the potent influence of mob psychology. For this reason, then, among others, a drama heard and seen under the usual conditions secures unique effects of response in contrast with the other sister forms of telling stories.

A heightening of effect upon auditor and spectator is gained—to mention one other advantage—by the fact that the story which in a work of fiction may extend to a length precluding the possibility of its reception at one sitting, may in the theater be brought within the compass of an evening, in the time between dinner and bed. This secures a unity of impression whereby the play is a gainer over the novel. A great piece of fiction like *David Copperfield*, or *Tom Jones*, or *A Modern Instance*, or *Alice for Short* cannot be read in a day, except as a feat of endurance and under unusual privileges of time to spare. But a great play—Shakespeare's *Hamlet* or Ibsen's *A Doll's House*—can be absorbed in its entirety in less than three hours, and while the hearer has perhaps not left his seat. Other things being equal, and whatever the losses, this establishes a superiority for the play. A coherent section of life, which is what the story should be, conveyed in the whole by this brevity of execution, so that the recipient may get a full sense of its organic unity, cannot but be more impressive than any medium of story telling where this is out of the question. The merit of the novel, therefore, supreme in its way, is another merit; "one star differeth from another in glory." It will be recalled that Poe, with this matter of brevity of time and unity of impression in mind, declared that there was no such thing as a long poem; meaning that only the short poem which could be read through at one sitting could attain to the highest effects.

But along with these advantages go certain limitations, too, in this form of story telling; limitations which warn the play not to encroach upon the domain of fiction, and which have much to do with making the form what it is.

From its very nature the novel can be more thorough-going in the delineation of character. The drama, as we have seen, must, under its stern restrictions of time, seize upon outstanding traits and assume that much of the development has taken place before the rise of the first curtain. The novel shows character in process of development; the play shows what character, developed to the point of test, will do when the test comes. Its method, especially in the hands of modern playwrights like Ibsen and Shaw, is to exhibit a human being acted upon suddenly by a situation which exposes the hidden springs of action and is a culmination of a long evolution prior to the plot that falls within the play proper.

In the drama characters must for the most part be displayed in external acts, since action is of the very essence of a play; in a novel, slowly and through long stretches of time, not the acts alone but the thoughts, motives and desires of the character may be revealed. Obviously, in the drama this cannot be done, in any like measure, in spite of the fact that some of the late psychologists of the drama, like Galsworthy, Bennett and others, have tried to introduce a more careful psychology into their play-making. At the best, only an approximation to the subtlety and penetration of fiction can be thus attained. It were wiser to recognize the limitation and be satisfied with the compensating gain of the more vivid, compelling effect secured through the method of presenting human beings, natural to the playhouse.

There are also arbitrary and artificial conventions of the stage conditioning the story which may perhaps be regarded as drawbacks where the story in fiction is freer in these respects. Both forms of story telling strive—never so eagerly as today—for a truthful representation of life. The stage, traditionally, in its depiction of character through word and action, has not been so close to life as fiction; the dialogue has been further removed from the actual idiom of human speech. It is only of late that stage talk in naturalness has begun to rival the verisimilitude of dialogue in the best fiction. This may well be for the reason (already touched upon) that the presence of the speakers on the stage has in itself a reality which corrects the artificiality of the words spoken. "I did not know," the theater auditor might be imagined as saying, "that people talked like that; but there they are, talking; it must be so."

The drama in all lands is trying as never before to represent life in speech as well as act; and the strain hitherto put upon the actor, who in the past had as part of his function to make the artificial and unreal plausible and artistic, has been so far removed as to enable him to give his main strength to genuine interpretation.

The time values on the stage are a limitation which makes for artificiality; actual time must of necessity be shortened, for if true chronology were preserved the play would be utterly balked in its purpose of presenting a complete story that, however brief, must cover more time than is involved in what is shown upon the boards of a theater. As a result all time values undergo a proportionate shrinkage. This can be estimated by the way meals are eaten on the stage. In actual life twenty minutes are allotted for the scamped eating time of the railway station, and we all feel it as a grievance. Half an hour is scant decency for the unpretentious private meal; and as it becomes more formal an hour is better, and several hours more likely. Yet no play could afford to allow twenty minutes for this function, even were it a meal of state; it would consume half an act, or thereabouts. Consequently, on the stage, the effect of longer time is produced by letting the audience see the general details of the feast; food eaten, wine drunk, servants waiting, and conversation interpolated. It is one of the demands made upon the actor's skill to make all these condensed and selected minutiæ of a meal stand for the real thing; once more art is rearranging life, under severe pressure. If those interested will test with watch in hand the actual time allowed for the banquet in *A Parisian Romance*, so admirably envisaged by the late Richard Mansfield, or the famous Thanksgiving dinner scene in *Shore Acres*, fragrantly associated with the memory of the late James A. Herne, they will possibly be surprised at the brevity of such representations.

Because of this necessary compression, a scale of time has to be adopted which shall secure an effect of actualness by a cunning obeyance of proportion; the reduction of scale is skillful, and so the result is congruous. And it is plain that fiction may take more time if it so desires in such scenes; although even in the novel the actual time consumed by a formal dinner would be reproduced by the novelist at great risk of boring his reader.

Again, with disadvantages in mind, it might be asserted that the stage story suffers in that some of the happenings involved in the plot must perforce transpire off stage; and when this is so there is an inevitable loss of effect, inasmuch as it is of the nature of drama, as has been noted, to show events, and the indirect narrative method is to be avoided as undramatic. Tyros in play-writing fail to make this distinction; and as a generalization it may be stated that whenever possible a play should show a thing, rather that state it. "Seeing is believing," to repeat the axiom. Yet a qualifier may here be made, for in certain kinds of drama or when a certain effect is striven for the indirect method may be powerfully effective. The murder in *Macbeth* gains rather than loses because it takes place outside the scene; Maeterlinck in his earlier Plays for Marionettes, so called, secured remarkable effects of suspense and tension by systematically using the principle of indirection; as where in *The Seven Princesses* the princesses who are the particular exciting cause of the play are not seen at all by the audience; the impression they make, a great one, comes through their effect upon certain characters on the stage and this heightens immensely the dramatic value of the unseen figures. We may point to the Greeks, too, in illustration, who in their great folk dramas of legend regularly made use of the principle of indirect narration when the aim was to put before the vast audiences the terrible occurrences of the fable, not *coram populo*, as Horace has it, not in the presence of the audience, but rather off stage. Nevertheless, these exceptions can be explained without violating the general principle that in a stage story it is always dangerous not to exhibit any action that is vital to the play. And this compulsion, it will be evident, is a restriction which may at times cripple the scope of the dramatist, while yet it stimulates his skill to overcome the difficulty.

Summarizing the differences which go to make drama distinctive as a story-telling form and distinguish it from other story molds: a play in contrast with fiction tells its tale by word, act and scene in a rising scale of importance, and within briefer time limits, necessitating a far more careful selection of material, and a greater emphasis upon salient moments in the handling of plot; and because of the device of act divisions, with certain moments of heightened interest culminating in a central scene and thus gaining in tension and intensity by this enforced method of compression and stress; while losing the opportunity to amplify and more carefully to delineate character. It gains as well because the story comes by the double receipt of the eye and ear to a theater audience some of whom at least, through illiteracy, might be unable to appreciate the story printed in a book. The play thus is the most democratic and popular form of story telling, and at the same time is capable of embodying, indeed has embodied, the greatest creative literature of various nations. And for a generation now, increasingly, in the European countries and in English-speaking lands, the play has begun to come into its own as an art form with unique advantages in the way of wide appeal and cultural possibilities.

Chapter 2

The Play, a Cultural Opportunity

Certain remarks at the close of the preceding chapter hint at what is in mind in giving a title to the present one. The play, this democratic mode of story telling, attracting vast numbers of hearers and universally popular because man is ever avid of amusement and turns hungrily to such a medium as the theater to satisfy a deeply implanted instinct for pleasure, can be made an experience to the auditor properly to be included in what he would call his cultural opportunity. That is to say, it can take its place among those civilizing agencies furnished by the arts and letters, travel and the higher aspects of social life. A drama, as this book seeks to show, is in its finest estate a work of art comparable with such other works of art as pictures, statuary, musical compositions and the achievements of the book world. I shall endeavor later to show a little more in detail wherein lie the artistic requirements and successes of the play; and a suggestion of this has been already made in chapter one.

But this thought of the play as a work of art has hardly been in the minds of folk of our race and speech until the recent awakening of an enlightened interest in things dramatic; a movement so brief as to be embraced by the present generation. The theater has been regarded carelessly, thoughtlessly, merely as a place of idle amusement, or worse; ignorant prejudice against it has been rife, with a natural reaction for the worse upon the institution itself. The play has neither been associated with a serious treatment of life nor with the refined pleasure derivable from contact with art. Nor, although the personality of actors has always been acclaimed, and an infinite amount of silly chatter about their private lives been constant, have theater-goers as a class realized the distinguished skill of the dramatist in the handling of a very difficult and delicate art, nor done justice to the art which the actor represents, nor to his own artistry in it. But now a change has come, happily. The English-speaking lands have begun at least to get into line with other enlightened countries, to comprehend the educational value of the playhouse, and the consequent importance of the play. The rapid growth today in what may be called social consciousness has quickened our sense of the social significance of an institution that, whatever its esthetic and intellectual status, is an enormous influence in the daily life of the multitude. Gradually those who think they have come to see that the theater, this people's pleasure, should offer drama that is rational, wholesome amusement; that society in general has a vital stake in the nature of an entertainment so widely diffused, so imperatively demanded and so surely effective in shaping the ideals of the people at large. The final chapter will enlarge upon this suggestion.

And this idea has grown along with the now very evident re-birth of a drama which, while practical stage material, has taken on the literary graces and makes so strong an appeal as literature that much of our best in letters is now in dramatic form: the play being the most notable contribution, after the novel, of our time. Leading writers everywhere are practical dramatists; men of letters, yet also men of the theater, who write plays not only to be read but to be acted, and who have conquered the difficult technique of the drama so as to kill two birds with the one stone.

The student of historical drama will perceive that this welcome change is but a return to earlier and better conditions when the mighty play-makers of the past—

Calderón, Molière, Shakespeare and their compeers—were also makers of literature which we still read with delight. And, without referring to the past, a glance at foreign lands will reveal the fact that other countries, if not our own, have always recognized this cultural value of the stage and hence given the theater importance in the civic or national life, often spending public moneys for its maintenance and using it (often in close association with music) as a central factor in national culture. The traveler today in Germany, France, Russia and the Scandinavian lands cannot but be impressed with this fact, and will bring home to America some suggestive lessons for patriotic native appreciation. In the modern educational scheme, then, room should be made for some training in intelligent play-going. So far from there being anything Quixotic in the notion, all the signs are in its favor. The feeling is spreading fast that school and college must include theater culture in the curriculum and people at large are seeking to know something of the significance of the theater in its long evolution from its birth to the present, of the history of the drama itself, of the nature of a play regarded as a work of art; of the specific values, too, of the related art of the actor who alone makes the drama vital; and of the relative excellencies, in the actual playhouses of our time, of plays, players and playwrights; together with some idea of the rapidly changing present-day conditions. Such changes include the coming of the one-act play, the startling development of the moving picture, the growth of the Little Theater, the rise of the masque and pageant, and so on with other manifestations yet. Surely, some knowledge in a field so broad and humanly appealing, both for legitimate enjoyment of the individual and in view of his obligations to fellow man, is of equal moment to a knowledge of the chemical effect of hydrochloric acid upon marble, or of the working of a table of logarithms. These last are less involved in the living of a normal human being.

Here are signs of the time, which mark a revolution in thought. In the light of such facts, it is curious to reflect upon the neglect of the theater hitherto for centuries as an institution and the refusal to think of the play as worthy until it was offered upon the printed page. The very fact that it was exhibited on the stage seemed to stamp it as below serious consideration. And that, too, when the very word *play* implies that it is something to be played. The taking over of the theaters by uneducated persons to whom such a place was, like a department store, simply an emporium of desired commodities, together with the Puritanic feeling that the playhouse, as such, was an evil thing frowned upon by God and injurious to man, combined to set this form of entertainment in ill repute. Bernard Shaw, in that brilliant little play, *The Dark Lady of the Sonnets*, sets certain shrewd words in the mouths of Shakespeare and Queen Elizabeth pertinent to this thought:

SHAKESPEARE: "Of late, as you know, the Church taught the people by means of plays; but the people flocked only to such as were full of superstitious miracles and bloody martyrdoms; and so the Church, which also was just then brought into straits by the policy of your royal father, did abandon and discountenance playing; and thus it fell into the hands of poor players and greedy merchants that had their pockets to look to and not the greatness of your kingdom."

ELIZABETH: "Master Shakespeare, you speak sooth; I cannot in anywise amend it. I dare not offend my unruly Puritans by making so lewd a place as the playhouse a public charge; and there be a thousand things to be done in this London of mine before your poetry can have its penny from the general purse. I tell thee, Master Will, it will be three hundred years before my subjects learn that man cannot live by bread alone, but by every word that cometh from the mouth of those whom God inspires."

The height of the incongruous absurdity was illustrated in the former teaching of Shakespeare. Here was a writer incessantly hailed as the master poet of the race; he bulked large in school and college, perforce. Yet the teacher was confronted by the embarrassing fact that Shakespeare was also an actor: a profession given over to the sons of Belial; and a playwright who actually wrote his immortal poetry in the shape of theater plays. This was sad, indeed! The result was that in both the older teaching and academic criticism emphasis was always placed upon Shakespeare the poet, the great mind; and Shakespeare the playwright was hardly explained at all; or if explained the illumination was more like darkness visible, because those in the seats of judgment were so ignorant of play technique and the requirements of the theater as to make their attempts well-nigh useless. It remained for our own time and scholars like George P. Baker and Brander Matthews, with intelligent, sympathetic comprehension of the play as a form of art and the playhouse as conditioning it, to study the Stratford bard primarily as playwright and so give us a new and more accurate portrait of him as man and creative worker.

I hope it is beginning to be apparent that intelligent play-going starts long before one goes to the theater. It means, for one thing, some acquaintance with the history of drama, and the theater which is its home, both in the development of English culture and that of other important nations whose dramatic contribution has been large. This aspect of culture will be enlarged upon in the following chapters. Much can be done—far more than has been done—in this historical survey in school and college to prepare American citizens for rational theater enjoyment. There is nothing pedantic in such preparation. Nobody objects to being sufficiently trained in art to distinguish a chromo from an oil masterpiece or to know the difference in music between a cheap organ-grinder jingle and the rhythmic marvels of a Chopin. It is equally foolish to be unable to give a reason for the preference for a play by Shaw or Barrie over the meaningless coarse farce by some stage hack. It is all in the day's culture and when once the idea that the theater is an art has been firmly seized and communicated to many all that seems bizarre in such a thought will disappear—and good riddance!

The first and fundamental duty to the theater is to attend the play worthy of patronage. If one be a theater-goer, yet has never taken the trouble to see a certain drama that adorns the playhouse, one is open to criticism. The abstention, when the chance was offered, must in fact either be a criticism of the play or of the person himself because he refrained from supporting it.

But let it be assumed that our theater-goer is in his seat, ready to do his part in the patronage of a good play. How, once there, shall he show the approval, or at least interest, his presence implies?

By making himself a part of the sympathetic psychology of the audience, as a whole; not resisting the effect by a position of intellectual aloofness natural to a human being burdened with the self-consciousness that he is a critic; but gladly recognizing the human and artistic qualities of the entertainment. Next, by giving external sign of this sympathetic approval by applause. Applause in this country generally means the clapping of the hands; only exceptionally, and in large cities, do we hear the *bravos* customary in Europe.

But suppose the play merit not approval but the reverse; what then? The gallery gods, those disthroned deities, were wont more rudely to supplement this manual testimony by the use of their other extremities, the feet. The effect, however, is not desirable. Yet, in respect of this matter of disapproval, it would seem as if the British in their frank booing of a piece which does not meet their wishes were exercising a valuable check upon bad drama. In the United States we signify positive approval, but not its negation. The result is that the cheaper element of an audience may applaud and so help the fate of a poor play, while the hostility of those better fitted to judge is unknown to all concerned with the fortunes of the drama, because it is thus silent. A freer use of the hiss, heard with us only under rare circumstances of provocation, might be a salutary thing, for this reason. An audible expression of reproof would be of value in the case of many unworthy plays.

But perhaps in the end the rebuke of non-attendance and the influence of the minatory word passed on to others most assists the failure of the play that ought to fail. If the foolish auditor approve where he should condemn, and so keep the bad play alive by his backing, the better view has a way of winning at the last. Certainly, for conspicuous success some qualities of excellence, if not all of them, must be present.

But intelligent play-going means also a perception of the art of acting, so that the technique of the player, not his personality, will command the auditor's trained attention and he will approve skill and frown upon its absence.

And while it is undoubtedly more difficult to convey this information educationally, the ideal way being to see the best acting early and late and to reflect upon it in the light of acknowledged principles, something can certainly be done to prepare prospective theater-goers for appreciation of the profession of the player; substituting for the blind, time-honored "I know what I like," the more civilized: "I approve it for the following good and sufficient reasons." Even in school, and still more in college, the teacher can cooperate with the taught by suggesting the plays to be seen, amateur as well as professional; and by classroom discussion afterward, not only of the plays but concerning their rendition. Students are quick to respond when this is done, for the vital object lesson of current drama always appeals to them, and they are glad to observe a connection between their amusement and their culture. At present, or at least up to a very recent time, the eccentricity of such a procedure would all but have endangered the position of the teacher so foolhardy as to act upon the assumption that the drama seen the night before could be in any way used to impart permanent lessons concerning a great art to the minds of the pupils. Luckily, a more liberal view is taking the place of this crass

Philistinism.

In a proper appreciation of the actor the hearer will look beyond the pulchritude of an actress or the fit of an actor's clothes; he will judge Miss Ethel Barrymore by her power of envisaging the part she assumes, and not be overly interested in an argument as to her increase of avoirdupois of late years. He will not allow himself to consume time over the question whether Mr. William Gillette in private life is addicted to chloral because Sherlock Holmes is a victim of that most reprehensible habit.

And above all he will constantly remind himself that acting is the art of impersonation, exactly that; and, therefore, just as high praise goes to the player who admirably portrays a disagreeable part as to one in whose mouth the playwright has set lines which make him beloved from curtain to curtain. Yet the majority of persons in a typical American theater audience hopefully confuse the part with the player, and award praise or blame according as they like or dislike the part itself.

The intelligent auditor will also give approval to the stage artist who, instead of drawing attention to himself by the use of exaggerated methods, quietly does his work, keeps always within the stage picture, and trusts to his truthful representation to secure conviction and reward. How common is it to see some player overstressing his part, who, instead of being boohed and hissed as he deserves and as he infallibly would be in some countries, receives but the more applause for his inexcusable overstepping of the modesty of his art. It becomes part of the duty of our intelligent play-goer to teach such pseudo-artists their place, for as long as they win the meed of ill-timed and ignorant approval, so long will they flourish.

Nor will the critic of the acceptable actor fail to observe that the latter prefers working for the ensemble—*team work*, in the sporting phrase—to that personal display disproportionate to the general effect which will always make the judicious grieve. In theatrical parlance, "hogging the stage" has flourished simply for the reason that it deceives a sufficient number in the seats to secure applause and so throws dust in the eyes of the general public as to its true iniquity. The actor is properly to be judged, not by his work detached from that of his fellows, but ever in relation to the totality of impression which means a play instead of a personal exhibition. It is his business to cooperate with others in a single effect in which each is a factor in the exact measure of the importance of his part as conceived by the dramatist. Where a minor part becomes a major one through the ability of a player, as in the famous case of the elder Sothern's Lord Dundreary, it is at the expense of the play; *Our American Cousin* was negligible as drama, and hence it did not matter. But if the drama is worth while, serious injury to dramatic art may follow.

Again, the intelligent play-goer will carefully distinguish in his mind between actor and playwright. Realizing that "the play's the thing," he will demand that even the so-called star (too often an actor foisted into prominence for a non-artistic reason) shall obey the laws of his art and those of drama, and not unduly minimize for personal reasons the work of his coadjutors in the play, nor that of the playwright who intended him to go so far and no further. The actor who, whatever his fame, and no matter how much an unthinking audience is complaisant when he does it, makes a practice of giving himself a center-of-the-stage prominence beyond what the drama calls for, is no artist, but a show man, neither more nor less, who deserves to be rated with the mountebanks rather than with the artists of his profession. But it may be feared that "stars" will continue to seek the stage center and crowd others of the cast out of the right focus, to say nothing of distorting the work of the dramatist, under the goad of megalomania, so long as a goodly number of unintelligent spectators egg him on. His favorite line of poetry will be that of Wordsworth:

"Fair as a star when only one is shining in the sky." It is to help the personnel of such an audience that our theater-goer needs his training.

A general realization of all this will definitely affect one's theater habit and make for the good of all that concerns the art of the playhouse. It will lead the properly prepared person to see a good play competently done, but with no supreme or far-famed actor in the company, in preference to a foolish play, or worse, carried by a "star"; or a play negligible as art or hopelessly *passé* as art or interpretation of life for which an all-star cast has been provided, as if to take the eye of the spectator off the weaknesses of the drama. Often a standard play revived by one of these hastily gathered companies of noted players resolves itself into an interest in individual performances which must lack that organic unity which comes of longer association. The opportunity afforded to get a true idea of the play is made quite secondary, and sometimes entirely lost sight of.

Nor will the trained observer in the theater be cheated by the dollar mark in his theatrical entertainment. He will come to feel that an adequate stock company, playing the best plays of the day, may afford him more of drama culture for an expenditure of fifty cents for an excellent seat than will some second-rate traveling company which presents a drama that is a little more recent but far less worthy, to see which the charge is three or four times that modest sum. All over the land today nominally cultivated folk will turn scornfully away from a fifty-cent show, as they call it, only because it is cheap in the literal sense, whereas the high-priced offering is cheap in every other sense but the cost of the seat. Such people overlook the nature of the play presented, the playwright's reputation, and the quality of the performance; incapable of judging by the real tests, they stand confessed as vulgarians and ignoramuses of art. We shall not have intelligent audiences in American theaters, speaking by and large, until theater-goers learn to judge dramatic wares by some other test than what it costs to buy them. Such a test is a crude one, in art, however infallible it may be in purely material commodities; indeed, is it not the wise worldling in other fields who becomes aware in his general bartering that it is unsafe to estimate his purchase exclusively by the price tag?

To one who in this way makes the effort to inform himself with regard to the things of the theater—plays, players and playwrights—concerning dramatic history both as it appertains to the drama and the theater; and concerning the intellectual as well as esthetical and human values of the theater-going experience, it will soon become apparent that it offers him cultural opportunity that is rich, wide and of ever deepening enjoyment. And taking advantage of it, he will dignify one of the most appealing pleasures of civilization by making it a part of his permanent equipment for satisfactory living.

Other aspects of this thought may now be expounded, beginning with a review of the play in its history; some knowledge of which is obviously an element in the complete appreciation of a theater evening. For the proper viewing of a given play one should have reviewed plays in general, as they constitute the body of a worthy dramatic literature.

Chapter 3

Up to Shakespeare

The recent vogue of plays like *The Servant in the House*, *The Passing of the Third Floor Back*, *The Dawn of Tomorrow*, and *Everywoman* sends the mind back to the early history of English drama and is full of instruction. Such drama is a reversion to type, it suggests the origin of all drama in religion. It raises the interesting question whether the blasé modern theater world will not respond, even as did the primitive audiences of the middle ages, to plays of spiritual appeal, even of distinct didactic purpose. And the suggestion is strengthened when the popularity is recalled of the morality play of *Everyman* a few years since, that being a revival of a typical mediæval drama of the kind. It almost looks as if we had failed to take into account the ready response of modern men and women to the higher motives on the stage; have failed to credit the substratum of seriousness in that chance collection of human beings which constitutes a theater audience. After all, they are very much like children, when under the influence of mob psychology; sensitive, plastic to the lofty and noble as they are to the baser suggestions that come to them across the footlights. In any case, these late experiences, which came by way of surprise to the professional purveyors of theatrical entertainment, give added emphasis to the statement that the stage is the child of mother church, and that the origin of drama in the countries whereof we have record is always religious. The mediæval beginnings in Europe and England have been described in their details by many scholars. Suffice it here to say that the play's birthplace is at the altar end of the cathedral, an extension of the regular service. The actors were priests, the audience the vast hushed throngs moved upon by incense, lights, music, and the intoned sacred words, and, for the touch of the dramatic which was to be the seed of a wonderful development, we may add some portion of the sacred story acted out by the stoled players and envisaged in the scenic pomp of the place. The lesson of the holy day was thus brought home to the multitude as it never would have been by the mere recital of the Latin words; scene and action lent their persuasive power to the natural associations of the church. Such is the source of modern drama; what was in the course of time to become "mere amusement," in the foolish phrase, began as worship; and if we go far back into the Orient, or to the southlying lands on the Mediterranean, we find in India and Greece alike this union of art and worship, whether the play began within church or temple or before Dionysian altars reared upon the green sward. The good and the beautiful, the esthetic and the spiritual, ever intertwined in the story of primitive culture.

And the gradual growth from this mediæval beginning is clear. First, a scenic elaboration of part of the service, centering in some portion of the life and death of Christ; then, as the scenic side grew more complex, a removal to the grounds outside the cathedral; an extension of the subject-matter to include a reverent treatment of other portions of the Bible narrative; next, the taking over of biblical drama by the guilds, or crafts, under the auspices of the patron saints of the various organizations, as when, on Corpus Christi day, one of the great saints' days of the year, a cycle of plays was presented in a town with the populace agog to witness it, and the movable vans followed each other at the street corners, presenting scene after scene of the story. Then a further extension of motives which admitted the use of the lives of the saints who presided over the guilds; and finally the further enlargement of theme due to the writing of drama of which the personages were abstract moral qualities, giving the name of Morality to this kind of play. Such, described with utter simplicity and brevity, was the interesting evolution.

Aside from all technicalities, and stripped of much of moment to the specialist, we have in this origin and early development a blend of amusement and instruction; a religious purpose linked with a frank recognition of the fact that if you make worship attractive you strengthen its hold upon mankind—a truth sadly lost sight of by the later Puritans. The church was wise, indeed, to unite these elements of life, to seize upon the psychology of the show and to use it for the purpose of saving souls. It was not until the sixteenth century and the immediate predecessors of Shakespeare that the play, under the influence of renaissance culture and the inevitable secularization of the theater in antagonism to the Puritan view of amusement, waxed worldly, and little by little lost the ear-marks of its holy birth and upbringing.

The day when the priests, still the actors of the play, walked down the nave and issued from the great western door of the cathedral, to continue the dramatic representations under the open sky, was truly a memorable one in dramatic history. The first instinct was not that of secularization, but rather the desire for freer opportunity to enact the sacred stories; a larger stage, more scope for dramatic action. Yet, although for generations the play remained religious in subject-matter and intent, it was inevitable that in time it should come to realize that its function was to body forth human life, unbounded by Bible themes: all that can happen to human beings on earth and between heaven and hell and beyond them, being fit material for treatment, since all the world's a stage, and flesh and blood of more vital interest to humanity at large than aught else. The rapid humanization of the religious material can be easily traced in the coarse satire and broad humor introduced into the Bible narratives: a free and easy handling of sacred scene and character natural to a more naïve time and by no means implying irreverence. Thus, in the Noah story, Mrs. Noah becomes a stout shrew whose unwillingness to come in out of the wet and bestow herself in dry quarters in the Ark must have been hugely enjoyed by the fifteenth century populace. And the Vice of the morality play degenerates into the clown of the performance, while even the Devil himself is made a cause for laughter.

Another significant step in the advance of the drama was made when the crafts took over the representations; for it democratized the show, without cheapening it or losing sight of its instructional nature. When the booths, or pageants as they were called, drew up at the crossing of the ways and performed their part in some story of didactic purport and broadly human, hearty, English atmosphere, with an outdoor flavor and decorative features of masque and pageantry, the spectators saw the prototype of the historic pageants which just now are coming again into favor. The drama of the future was shaping in a matrix which was the best possible to assure a long life, under popular, natural conditions. These conditions were to be modified and distorted by other, later additions from the cultural influence of the past and under the domination of literary traditions; but here was the original mold.

The method of presentation, too, had its sure effect upon the theater which was to follow this popular folk beginning. The movable van, set upon wheels, with its space beneath where behind a curtain the actors changed their costumes, suggests in form and upfitting the first primitive stages of the playhouses erected in the second half of the sixteenth century. Since but one episode or act of the play was to be given, there was no need of a change of scene, and the stage could be simple accordingly. Contemporary cuts show us the limited dimensions, the shallow depth and the bareness of accessories typical of this earliest of the housings of the drama, for such it might fairly be called. Obviously, on such a stage, the manner and method of portrayal are strictly defined: done out of doors, before a shifting multitude of all classes, with no close cohesion or unity, since another part of the story was told in another spot, the play, to get across—not the footlights, for there were none—but the intervening space which separated actors and audience, must be conveyed in broad simple outline and in graphic episodes, the very attributes which today, despite all subtleties and finesse, can be relied upon to bring response from the spectators in a theater. It must have been a great event when, in some quiet English town upon a day significant in church annals, the players' booths began their cycle, and the motley crowd gathered to hear the Bible narratives familiar to each and all, even as the Greek myths which are the stock material of the Greek drama were known to the vast concourse in the hillside theater of that day. In effect the circus had come to town, and we may be sure every urchin knew it and could be found open-mouthed in the front row of spectators. No possibility here of subtlety and less of psychologic morbidity. The beat of the announcing drum, the eager murmur of the multitude, the gay costumes and colorful booth, all ministered to the natural delight of the populace in show and story. The fun relieved the serious matter, and the serious matter made the fun acceptable. With no shift of scenery, the broadest liberty, not to say license, in the particulars of time and place were practiced; the classic unities were for a later and more sophisticate drama. There was no curtain and therefore no entr'act to interrupt the two hours' traffic of the stage; the play was continuous in a sense other than the modern.

As a result of these early conditions, the English play was to show through its history a fluidity, a plastic adaptation of material to end, in sharp contrast with other nations, the French, for one, whose first drama was enacted in a tennis court of fixed location, deep perspective and static scenery.

On the holy days which, as the etymology shows, were also holidays from the point of view of the crowd, drama was vigorously purveyed which made the primitive appeals of pathos, melodrama, farce and comedy. The actors became secular, but for long they must have been inspired with a sense of moral obligation in their work; a beautiful survival of which is to be seen at Oberammergau today. And the play itself remained religious in content and intention for generations after it had walked out of the church door. The church took alarm at last, aware that an instrument of mighty potency had been taken out of its hands. It is not surprising to find various popes passing edicts against this new and growingly influential form of public entertainment. It seemed to be on the way to become a rival. This may well have had its effect in the rapid taking over of the drama by the guilds, as later it was adopted by still more worldly organizations.

It was not from the people that the change to complete secularization of subject-matter and treatment came; but from higher cultural sources: from the schools and universities, touched by renaissance influences; as where Bishop Still produced *Gammer Gurton's Needle* for school use, the first English comedy; or from court folk, as when Lord Buckhurst with his associate, Sackville, wrote the frigid *Gorbudoc* based on the Senecan model and honorable historically because it is the first English tragedy. The play of Plautian derivation, *Ralph Roister Doister*, our first comedy of intrigue, is another example of cultural influences which came in to modify the main stream of development from the folk plays.

This was in the sixteenth century, but for over two

centuries the genuine English play had been forming itself in the religious nursery, as we saw. Now these other exotic and literary influences began to blend with the native, and the story of the drama becomes therefore more complex. The school and the court, classic literature and that of mediæval Europe, which represented the humanism it begot, fast qualified the product. But the straightest, most natural issue from the naïve morality and miracle genre is the robustious melodrama illustrated by such plays as Kyd's *Spanish Tragedy* and Marlowe's *Edward II*; which in turn lead directly on to Shakespeare's *Titus Andronicus*, *Hamlet* and chronicle history drama like *Richard III*; and on the side of farce, *Gammer Gurton's Needle*, so broadly English in its fun, is in the line of descent. And in proportion as the popular elements of rhetoric, show and moralizing were retained, was the appeal to the general audience made, and the drama genuinely English.

Up to 1576 we are concerned with the history of the drama and there is no public theater in the sense of a building erected for theatrical performances. After the strolling players with their booths, plays were given in scholastic halls, in schools and in private residences; while the more democratic and direct descendant of the pageants is to be seen in the inn yards where the stable end of the courtyard, inclosed on three sides by its parallelogram of galleries, is the rudimentary plan for the Elizabethan playhouse, when it comes, toward the end of the sixteenth century. But with the year 1576 and the erection in Shoreditch of the first Theater on English soil—so called, because it had no rivals and the name was therefore distinctive—the proper history of the institution begins. It marks a most important forward step in dramatic progress.

There is significance in the phrase descriptive of this first building; it was set up "in the fields," as the words run: which means, beyond city limits, for the city fathers, increasingly Puritan in feeling, looked dubiously upon an amusement already so much a favorite with all classes; it might prove a moral as well as physical plague spot by its crowding together of a heterogeneous multitude within pent quarters. Once started, the theater idea met with such hospitable reception that these houses were rapidly increased, until by the century's end half a dozen of the curious wooden hexagonal structures could be seen on the southward bank of the Thames, near the water, central in interest as we now look back upon them being The Globe, built in 1599 from the material of the demolished Shoreditch playhouse, and famed forever as Shakespeare's own house. Here at three o'clock of the afternoon upon a stage open to the sky and with the common run of spectators standing in the pit where now lounge the luxuriant occupants of orchestra seats, while those of the better sort sat on the stage or in the boxes which flanked the sides of the house and suggested the inn galleries of the earlier arrangement, were first seen the robust predecessors of Shakespeare, Marlowe, and Kyd and Peele and Nash; and later, Shakespeare, Beaumont and Fletcher, Ben Jonson and the other immortals whose names are names to conjure with, even to this day. Played in the daylight, and most crudely lighted, the play was deprived of the illusion produced by modern artificial light, and the stage, projecting far down into the audience, made equally impossible the illusion of the proscenium arch, a picture stage set apart from life and constituting a world of its own for the representation of the mimic story. There was small need for make-up on the part of the actors, since the garish light of day is a sad revealer of grease paint and powder; and the flaring cressets of oil that did service as footlights must, it would seem, have made darkness visible, when set beside the modern devices. It is plain enough that under these conditions a performance of a play in the particulars of seeing and hearing must have been seriously limited in effect. To reach the audience must have meant an appeal that was broadly human, and essentially dramatic. Fine language was indispensable; and a language drama is exactly what the Elizabethan theater gives us. Compelling interest of story, skillful mouthing of splendid poetry, virile situations that contained the blood and thunder elements always dear to the heart of the groundlings, these the play of that period had to have to hold the audiences. Impudent breakings in from the gentles who lounged on the stage and blew tobacco smoke from their pipes into the faces perchance of Burbage and Shakespeare himself; vulgar interpolations of some clown while the stage waited the entrance of a player delayed in the tiring room must have been daily occurrences. And yet, from such a stage, confined in extent and meager in fittings, and under such physical limitations of comfort and convenience, were the glories of the master poet given forth to the world. Our sense of the wonder of his work is greatly increased when we get a visualized comprehension of the conditions under which he accomplished it. It is well to add that one of the most fruitful phases of contemporary scholarship is that which has thrown so much light upon the structure of the first English theaters. We now realize as never before the limits of the scenic representation and the necessary restriction consequent upon the style of drama given.

Another interesting and important consideration should also be noted here; and one too generally overlooked. The groundlings in the pit, albeit exposed to wind and weather and deprived of the seats which minister to man's ease and presumably dispose him to a better reception of the piece, were yet in a position to witness the play as a play superior to that of the more aristocratic portions of the assemblage. However charming it may have been for the sprigs of the nobility to touch elbows with Shakespeare on the boards as he delivered the tender lines of old Adam in *As You Like It*, or to exchange a word aside with Burbage just before he began the immortal soliloquy, "To be or not to be," it is certain that these gentry were not so advantageously placed to enjoy the rendition as a whole as were master Butcher or Baker at the front. And it would seem reasonable to believe that the nature of the Elizabethan play, so broadly humorous, so richly romantic, so large and obvious in its values and languaged in a sort of surplusage of exuberance, is explained by the fact that it was the common herd to whom in particular the play was addressed in these early playhouses: not the literature in which it was written so much as the unfolding story and the tout ensemble which they were in a favorable position to take in. To the upper-class attendant at the play the unity of the piece must have been less dominant. And surely this must have tended to shape the play, to make it a democratic people's product. For it is an axiom that the dominant element in an audience settles the fate of a play.

But this new plaything, the theater, was not only the physical embodiment of the drama, it became a social institution as well. Nor was it without its evils. The splendors of Elizabethan literature have often blinded criticism to the more sleazy aspects of the problem. But investigation has made apparent enough that the Puritan attitude toward the new institution was not without its excuse. As we have seen, from the very first a respectable middle class element of society looked askance at the playhouse, and while this view became exaggerated with the growth of Puritanism in England, there is nothing to be gained in idealizing the stage conditions of that time, nor, more broadly, to deny that the manner of life involved and in some regards the nature of the appeal at any period carry with them the likelihood of license and of dissipation. The actor before Shakespeare's day had little social or legal status; and despite all the leveling up of the profession due to him and his associates, the "strolling player" had to wait long before he became the self-respecting and courted individuality of our own day. Women did not act during the Elizabethan period, nor until the Restoration; so that one of the present possibilities of corruption was not present. But on the other hand, the stage was without the restraining, refining influence of their presence; a coarser tone could and did prevail as a result. The fact that ladies of breeding wore masks at the theater and continued to do so into the eighteenth century speaks volumes for the public opinion of its morals; and the scholar who knows the wealth of idiomatic foulness in the best plays of Shakespeare, luckily hidden from the layman in large measure, does not need to be told of the license and lewdness prevalent at the time. The Puritans are noted for their repressive attitude toward worldly pleasures and no doubt part of their antagonism to the playhouse was due to the general feeling that it is a sin to enjoy oneself, and that any institution which was thronged by society for avowed purposes of entertainment must derive from the devil. But documentary evidence exists to show that an institution which in England made possible the drama of Shakespeare, Beaumont and Fletcher, Webster, Ford, Jonson and Dekkar, writings which we still point to with pride as our chief contribution to the creative literature of the world, could include abuses so flagrant as to call forth the stern denunciations of a Cromwell, and later even shock the decidedly easy standards of a Pepys. The religious element in society was, at intervals, to break out against the stage from pulpit or through the pen, in historical iteration of this early attitude; as with Collier in his famed attack upon its immorality at the close of the seventeenth century, and numerous more modern diatribes from such clergymen as Spurgeon and Buckley.

And in order to understand the peculiar relation of the respectable classes in America to the theater, it is necessary to realize that those cherishing this antipathy were our forefathers, the Puritan settlers. The attitude was inimical, and of course the circumstances were all against a proper development of the function of the playhouse. Art and letters upon American soil, forsooth, had to await their day in the seventeenth and following centuries, when our ancestors had to give their full strength to more utilitarian matters, or to the grave demands of the future life. The Anglo-Saxon notion that the theater is evil is to be traced directly to these historic causes; and transplanted to so favorable a soil as America, it has produced most unfortunate results in our dramatic history, the worst of all being the general unenlightened view respecting the use and usufruct of an institution in its nature capable of so much good alike to the masses and the classes.

Chapter 4

Growth to the Nineteenth Century

Preparedness in the appreciation of a modern play presupposes a knowledge of the origin and early development of English drama, as briefly sketched in the preceding pages. It also, and more obviously, involves some acquaintance with the master dramatists who led up to or flourished in the Elizabethan period, with Shakespeare as the central figure; it must, too, be cognizant of the gradual deterioration of the product in the post-Elizabethan time; of the temporary close of the public theaters under Puritan influence during the Commonwealth; and of the substitution for the mighty poetry of Shakespeare and his mates of the corrupt Restoration comedy which was introduced into England with the return of the second Stuart to the throne in 1660. This brilliant though brutally indecent comedy of manners, with Congreve, Wycherley, Etherage, Vanbrugh and Farquhar as chief playwrights, while it represents in literature the moral nadir of the polite section of English society, is of decided importance in our dramatic history, because it reflected the manners and morals of the time, and quite as much because it is conspicuous for skillful characterization, effective dialogue and a feeling for scene and situation—all elements in good dramaturgy. This intelligent attempt to know what lies historically behind present drama will also make itself aware of the falling away early in the eighteenth century, in favor of the new literary form, the Novel; and the all too brief flashing forth of another comedy of manners with Sheridan and Goldsmith, which retained the sparkle, wit and literary flavor of the Restoration, with a later decency and a wholesomer social view; to be followed again by a well-nigh complete divorce of literature and the stage until well past the middle of the nineteenth century, when began the gradual re-birth of a drama which once more took on the quality of letters and made a serious appeal as an esthetic art and a worthy interpretation of life: what may be called the modern school initiated by Ibsen.

All this interesting growth and wonderfully varied accomplishment may be but lightly touched upon here, for admirable studies of the different periods and schools by many scholars are at hand and the earnest theater student may be directed thereto for further reading. The work of Professor Schelling on Elizabethan drama is thorough and authoritative. The modern view of Shakespeare and his contribution (referred to in Chapter III) will be found in Professor Baker's *Development of Shakespeare as a Dramatist* and Professor Matthews' *Shakespeare as a Playwright*. The general reader will find in The Mermaid Series of plays good critical treatment of the main Elizabethan and post-Elizabethan plays, together with the texts, so that a practical acquaintance with the product may be gained. The series also includes the Restoration dramas in their best examples. For the Sheridan-Goldsmith plays a convenient edition is that in the Drama section of the Belles Lettres series of English Literature, where the representative plays of an author are printed with enlightening introductions and other critical apparatus. In becoming familiar with these aids the reader will receive the necessary hints to a further acquaintance with the more technical books which study the earlier, more difficult part of dramatic evolution, and give attention to the complex story of the development of the theater as an institution.

A few things stand out for special emphasis here in regard to this developmental time. Let it be remembered that the story of English drama in its unfolding should be viewed in twin aspects: the growth of the play under changing conditions; and the growth of the playhouse which makes it possible. What has been said already of the physical framework of the early English theater throws light at once, as we saw, upon the nature of the play. And in fact, throughout the development, the play has changed its form in direct relation to the change in the nature of the stage upon which the play has been presented. The older type is a stage suitable for the fine-languaged, boldly charactered, steadily presented play of Shakespeare acted on a jutting platform where the individual actor inevitably is of more prominence, and so poorly lighted and scantily provided with scenery that words perforce and robustious effects of acting were necessitated, instead of the scenic appeals, subtler histrionism and plastic face and body work of the modern stage which has shrunk back to become a framed-in picture behind the proscenium arch. As the reader makes himself familiar with Marlowe, who led on to Shakespeare, with the comedy and masque of Ben Jonson, with the romantic and social plays of Beaumont and Fletcher, the lurid tragic writing of Webster, the softer tragedy of Ford and the rollicking folk comedy, pastoral poetry or serious social studies of Dekkar and Heywood, he will come to realize that on the one hand what he supposed to be the sole touch of Shakespeare in poetic expression was largely a general gift of the spacious days of Elizabeth, poetry, as it were, being in the very air men breathed (A fact humorously yet keenly suggested in Bernard Shaw's clever piece, The Dark Lady of the Sonnets.); and yet will recognize that the Stratford man walked commonly on the heights only now and again touched by the others. And as he reads further the plays of dramatists like Massinger, Tourneur, Shirley, and Otway he will find, along with gleams and glimpses of the grand manner, a steady degeneration from high poetry and tragic seriousness to rant, bombast, and the pseudo-poetry that is rhetoric, with the declension of tragedy into melodrama. High poetry gradually disintegrates, and the way is prepared for the Restoration comedy.

In reflecting upon the effect of a closing of the public theaters for nearly twenty years (1642-1660) the student will appreciate what a body blow this must have been to the true interests of the stage; and find in it at least a partial explanation of the rebound to the vigorous indecencies of Congreve and his associates (Wycherley, Etherage, Vanbrugh, Farquhar) when the ban was removed; human nature, pushed too far, ever expressing itself by reactions.

The ineradicable and undeniable literary virtues of the Restoration writers and their technical advancement of the play as a form and a faithful mirror of one phase of English society will reconcile the investigator to a picture of life in which every man is a rake or cuckold and every woman a light o' love; a sort of boudoir atmosphere that has a tainted perfume removing it far from the morning freshness of the Elizabethans. And consequently he will experience all the more gratitude in reaching the eighteenth century plays: *The School for Scandal*, *The Rivals*, and *She Stoops to Conquer*, when they came a generation later. While retaining the polish and the easy carriage of good society, these dramas got rid of the smut and the smirch, and added a flavor of hearty English fun and a saner conception of social life; a drama rooted firmly in the fidelities instead of the unfaithfulnesses of human character. These eighteenth century plays, like those of the Restoration—*The Plain Dealer*, *The Way of the World*, *The Man of Mode*, *The Relapse*, and *The Beaux Stratagem*—were still played in the old-fashioned playhouses, like Drury Lane, or Covent Garden, with the stage protruding into the auditorium and the classic architecture ill adapted to acoustics, and the boxes so arranged as to favor aristocratic occupants rather than in the interests of the play itself. The frequent change of scene, the five-act division of form, the prologue and epilogue and the free use of such devices as the soliloquy and aside remind us of the subsequent advance in technique. These marks of a by-gone fashion we are glad to overlook or accept, in view of the essential dramatic values and permanent contribution to letters which Sheridan and Goldsmith made to English comedy. But at the same time it is only common sense to felicitate ourselves that these methods of the past have been outgrown, and better methods substituted. And we shall never appreciate eighteenth century play-making to the full until we understand that the authors wrote in protest against a sickly sort of unnatural sentimentality, mawkish and untrue to life, which had become fashionable on the English stage in the hands of Foote, Colman and others. Sheridan brought back common sense and Goldsmith dared to introduce "low" characters and laughed out of acceptance the conventional separation of the socially high and humble in English life. His preface to *The Good Natured Man* will be found instructive reading in relation to this service.

From 1775 to 1860 the English stage, looked back upon from the vantage point of our time, appears empty, indeed. It did not look so barren, we may believe, to contemporaries. Shakespeare was doctored to suit a false taste; so great an actor-manager as Garrick complacently playing in a version of *Lear* in which the ruined king does not die and Cordelia marries Edgar; an incredible prettification and falsification of the mighty tragedy! Jonson writes for the stage, though the last man who should have done so. Sheridan Knowles, in the early nineteenth century, gives us *Virginius*, which is still occasionally heard, persisting because of a certain vigor and effectiveness of characterization, though hopelessly old-fashioned in its rhetoric and its formal obeyance of outworn conventions, both artistic and intellectual. The same author's *The Honeymoon* is also preserved for us through possessing a good part for the accomplished actress. Later Bulwer, whose feeling for the stage cannot be denied, in *Money*, *Richelieu*, and *The Lady of Lyons*, shows how a certain gift for the theatrical, coupled with less critical standards, will combine to preserve dramas whose defects are now only too apparent.

As the nineteenth century advances the fiction of Reade and Dickens is often fitted to the boards and the fact that the latter was a natural theater man gave and still gives his product a frequent hearing on the stage. To meet the beloved characters of this most widely read of all English fictionists is in itself a pleasure sufficient to command generous audiences. Boucicault's *London Assurance* is good stage material rather than literature. Tom Taylor produced among many stage pieces a few of distinct merit; his *New Men and Old Acres* is still heard, in the hands of experimental amateurs, and reveals sterling qualities of characterization and structure.

But the fact remains, hardly modified by the sporadic manifestations, that the English stage was frankly separating itself from English literature, and by 1860 the divorce was practically complete. There was a woful lack of public consideration for its higher interests on the one hand, and no definite artistic endeavor to produce worthy stage literature on the other. Authors who wrote for the stage got no encouragement to print their dramas and so make the literary appeal; there was among them no esprit de corps, binding them together for a self-conscious effort to make the theater a place where literature throve and art maintained its sovereignty. No leading or representative writers were dramatists first of all. If such wrote plays, they did it half heartedly, and as an exercise rather than a practical aim. It is curious to ask ourselves if this falling away of the stage might not have been checked had Dickens given himself more definitely to dramatic writing. His bias in that direction is well known. He wrote plays in his younger days and was throughout his life a fine amateur actor: the dramatic and often theatric character of his fiction is familiar. It was his intention as a youth to go on the stage. But he chose the novel and perhaps in so doing depleted dramatic history.

Literature and the stage, then, had at the best a mere bowing acquaintance. Browning, who under right conditions of encouragement might have trained himself to be a theater poet, was chagrined by his experience with *The Blot on the 'Scutcheon* and thereafter wrote closet plays rather than acting drama. Swinburne, master of music and mage of imagination, was in no sense a practical dramatist. Shelley's dramas are also for book reading rather than stage presentation, in spite of the fact that his *Cenci* has theater possibilities to make one regret all the more his lack of stage knowledge and aim. Bailey's *Festus* is not an acting play, though it was acted; the sporadic drama, in fact, between 1850 and 1870, light or serious, was frankly literary in the academic sense and not adapted to stage needs; or else consisted of book dramatizations from Reade and Dickens; or simply represented the journeymen work of prolific authors with little or no claim to literary pretensions.

The practical proof of all this can be found in the absence of drama of the period in book form, except for the acting versions, badly printed and cheaply bound, which did not make the literary appeal at all. Where today our leading dramatists publish their work as a matter of course, offering it as they would fiction or any other form of literature, the reading public of the middle century neither expected nor received plays as part of their mental pabulum, and an element in the contemporary letters. The drama had not only ceased to be a recognized section of current literature, but was also no longer an expression of national life. The first faint gleam of better things came when T. W. Robertson's genteel light comedies began to be produced at the Court Theater in 1868. As we read or see *Caste* or *Society* today they seem somewhat flimsy material, to speak the truth; and their technique, after the rapid development of a generation, has a mechanical creak for trained ears. But we must take them at the psychologic moment of their appearance, and recognize that they were a very great advance on what had gone before. They brought contemporary social life upon the stage as did Congreve in 1680, Sheridan in 1765; and they made that life interesting to large numbers of theater-goers who hitherto had abstained from play acting. And so *Caste* and its companion plays, of which it is the best, drew crowded houses and the stage became once more an amusement to reckon with in polite circles. The royal box was once more occupied, the playhouse became fashionable, no longer quite negligible as a form of art. To be sure, this was a town drama, and for the upper classes, as was the Restoration Comedy and that of the eighteenth century. It was not a people's theater, the Theater Robertson, but it had the prime merit of a more truthful representation of certain phases of the life of its day. And hence Robertson will always be treated as a figure of some historical importance in the British drama, though not a great dramatist.

In the eighteen eighties another influence began to be felt, that of Ibsen. The great dramatist from the North was made known to English readers by the criticism and translations of Gosse and Archer; and versions of his plays were given, tentatively and occasionally, in England, as in other lands. Thus readers and audiences alike gradually came to get a sense of a new force in the theater: an uncompromisingly truthful, stern portrayal of modern social conditions, the story told with consummate craftsmanship, and the national note sounding beneath the apparent pessimism. Here were, it was evident, new material, new method and a new insistence upon intellectual values in the theater. It can now be seen plainly enough that Ibsen's influence upon the drama of the nineteenth century is commensurate in revolutionary results with that of Shakespeare in the sixteenth. He gave the play a new and improved formula for play-writing; and he showed that the theater could be used as an arena for the discussion of vital questions of the day. Even in France, the one country where dramatic development has been steadily important for nearly three centuries, his influence has been considerable; in other European lands, as in England, his genius has been a pervasive force. Whether he will or no, the typical modern dramatist is a son of Ibsen, in that he has adopted the Norwegian's technique and taken the function of playwright more seriously than before.

Both with regard to intellectual values and technique, then, it is no exaggeration to speak of the modern drama, although it be an expression of the spirit of the time in reflecting social evolution, as bearing the special hallmark of Ibsen's influence. A word follows on the varied and vital accomplishment of the present period.

Chapter 5

The Modern School

We have noted that Ibsen's plays began to get a hearing in England in the Eighteen-Nineties. In fact, it was in 1889 that Mr. J. T. Grein had the temerity to produce at his Independent Theater in London *A Doll's House*, and followed it shortly afterward by the more drastic *Ghosts*. The influence in arousing an interest in and knowledge of a kind of drama which entered the arena for the purpose of social challenge and serious satiric attack was incalculable. Both Jones and Pinero, honorable pioneers in the making of the new English drama, and still actively engaged in their profession, had begun to write plays some years before this date; but it may be believed that the example of Ibsen, if not originating their impulse, was part of the encouragement to let their own work reflect more truthfully the social time spirit and to study modern character types with closer observation, allowing their stories to be shaped not so much by theatric convention as by honest psychologic necessity.

Jones began with melodrama, of which *The Silver King* (1882), *Saints and Sinners* (1884) and *The Middle Man* (1889) are examples; Pinero with ingenious farces happily associated with the fortunes of Sir Squire Bancroft and his wife, *The Magistrate* (1885) being an excellent illustration of the type. The dates are significant in showing the turning of these skillful playwrights to play-making that was more serious in the handling of life and more artistic in constructive values; they are practically synchronous with the introduction of Ibsen into England. Both authors have now long lists of plays to their credit, with acknowledged masterpieces among them. Pinero's earlier romantic style may be seen in the enormously successful *Sweet Lavender*, a style repeated ten years later in *Trelawney of the Wells*; his more mature manner being represented in *The Second Mrs. Tanqueray*, the best of a number of plays which center in the woman who is a social rebel, the dramatist's tone being almost austerely grim in carrying the study to its logical conclusion. For a time Sir Arthur seemed to be preoccupied with the soiled dove as dramatic inspiration; but so fine a recent play as *The Thunderbolt* shows he can get away from it. Jones' latest and best work as well has a tendency to the serious satiric showing-up of the failings of prosperous middle-class English society; this, however, in the main, kept in abeyance to story interest and constructive skill in its handling: *Mrs. Dane's Defense, The Case of Rebellious Susan, The Liars, The Rogue's Comedy, The Hypocrites*, and *Michael and His Lost Angel* stand for admirably able performances in different ways.

At the time when these two dramatists were beginning to produce work that was to change the English theater Bernard Shaw, after writing several pieces of fiction, had begun to give his attention to plays so advanced in technique and teaching that he was forced to wait more than a decade to get a wide hearing in the theater. His debt to the Norwegian has been handsomely acknowledged by the Irish dramatist, wit and philosopher who was to become the most striking phenomenon of the English theater: with all the differences, an English Ibsen. A little later, in the early eighteen nineties, another brilliant Irishman, Oscar Wilde, wrote a number of social comedies whose playing value today testifies to his gift in telling a stage story, while his epigrammatic wit and literary polish gave them the literary excellence likely to perpetuate his name. For the comedy of manners, light, easy, elegant, keen, and with satiric point in its reflection of society, nothing of the time surpasses such dramas as *Lady Windermere's Fan* and *A Woman of No Importance*. The author's farce—farce, yet more than farce in dialogue and characterization—*The Importance of Being Earnest*, is also a genuine contribution in its kind. And the strange, somber, intensely poetic *Salome* is a remarkable *tour de force* in an unusual field.

The tendency to turn from fiction to the drama as another form of story telling fast coming into vogue is strikingly set forth and embellished in the case of Sir James Barrie, who, after many successes in novel and short story, became a dramatist some twenty years ago and is now one of the few men of genius writing for the stage. His *Peter Pan, The Little Minister, The Admirable Crichton*, and *What Every Woman Knows* are four of over a dozen dramas which have given him world fame. Uniquely, among English writers whose work is of unquestionable literary quality, he refrains from the publication of plays; a very regrettable matter to countless who appreciate his rare quality. He is in his droll way of whimsy a social critic beneath the irresponsible play of a poet's fancy and an idealist's vision. His keen yet gentle interpretations of character are solidly based on truth to the everlasting human traits, and his poetry is all the better for its foundation of sanity and its salt of wit. One has an impulse to call him the Puck of the English theater; then feels compelled to add a word which recognizes the loving wisdom mingling with the pagan charm. Sir James is as unusual in his way as Shaw in his. Of late he has shown an inclination to write brief, one-act pieces, thereby adding to our interest in a form of drama evidently just beginning to come into greater regard.

For daring originality both of form and content Bernard Shaw is easily the first living dramatist of England. He is a true son of Ibsen, in that he insists on thinking in the theater, as well as in the experimental nature of his technique, which has led him to shape for himself the drama of character and thesis he has chosen to write. To the thousands who know his name through newspaper publicity or the vogue of some piece of his in the playhouse, Shaw is simply a witty Irishman, dealer in paradox and wielder of a shillelah swung to break the heads of Philistines for the sheer Celtic love of a row. To the few, however, an honorable minority now rapidly increasing, he is a deeply earnest, constructive social student and philosopher, who uses a popular amusement as a vehicle for the wider dissemination of perfectly serious views: a socialist, a mystic who believes in the Life Force sweeping man on (if man but will) to a high destiny, and a lover of fellow man who in his own words regards his life as belonging to the community and wishes to serve it, in order that he may be "thoroughly used up" when he comes to die. He has conquered as a playwright because beneath the sparkling sally, the startling juxtaposition of character and the apparent irreverence there hides a genuinely religious nature. Shaw shows himself an "immoralist" only in the sense that he attacks jejune, vicious pseudo-morals now existent. For sheer acting values in the particulars of dialogue, character, scenic effectiveness, feeling for climax and unity of aim such plays as *Candida, Arms and the Man, Captain Brassbound's Profession, The Devil's Disciple, John Bull's Other Island, Man and Superman, The Showing Up of Blanco Posnett,* and others yet, are additions to the serious comedy of England likely to be of lasting luster, so far as contemporary vision can penetrate.

One of the most interesting developments of recent years has been the Irish theater movement, in itself part of the general rehabilitation of the higher imaginative life of that remarkable people. The drama of the gentle idealist poet Yeats, of the shrewdly observant Lady Gregory and of the grimly realistic yet richly romantic Synge has carried far beyond their little country, so that plays like Yeats' *The Land of Heart's Desire* and *The Hour Glass*, Lady Gregory's *Spreading the News* and Synge's *Riders to the Sea* and *The Playboy of the Western World* are heard wherever the English language is understood, this stage literature being aided in its travels by the excellent company of Irish Players founded to exploit it and giving the world a fine example of the success that may come from a single-eyed devotion to an ideal: namely, the presentation for its own sake of the simple typical native life of the land.

It should be remembered that while these three leaders are best known, half a dozen other able Irish dramatists are associated with them, and doing much to interpret the farmer or city folk: writers like Mayne, Boyle, McComas, Murray, and Robinson.

Under the stimulus of Shaw in his reaction against the machine-made piece and the tiresome reiteration of sex motives, there has sprung up a younger school which has striven to introduce more varied subject-matter and a broader view, also greater truth and subtler methods in play-making. Here belong Granville Barker, with his *Voysey Inheritance* (his best piece), noteworthy also as actor-manager and producer; the novelists, Galsworthy and Bennett; and Masefield, whose *Tragedy of Nan* contains imaginative poetry mingled with melodrama; and still later figures, conspicuous among them the late Stanley Houghton, whose *Hindle Wakes* won critical and popular praise; others being McDonald Hastings with *The New Sin*; Githa Sowerby, author of the grim, effective play, *Rutherford and Son*; Elizabeth Baker, with *Chains* to her credit; Wilfred Gibson, who writes brief poignant studies of east London in verse that in form is daringly realistic; Cosmo Hamilton, who made us think in his attractive *The Blindness of Virtue*; and J. O. Francis, whose Welsh play, *Change*, was recognized as doing for that country the same service as the group led by Yeats and Synge has performed for Ireland.

A later Synge seems to have arisen in Lord Dunsany,

whose dramas in book form have challenged admiration; and since his early death St. John Hankin's dramatic work is coming into importance as a masterly contribution to light comedy, the sort of drama that, after the Wilde fashion, laughs at folly, satirizes weakness, refrains from taking sides, and never forgets that the theater should offer amusement.

Of all these playwrights, rising or risen, who have got a hearing after the veterans first mentioned, Galsworthy seems most significant for the profound social earnestness of his thought, the great dignity of his art and the fact that he rarely fails to respect the stage demand for objective interest and story appeal. Some of these new dramatists go too far in rejecting almost scornfully the legitimate theater mood of amusement and the necessity of a method differing from the more analytic way of fiction. Mr. Galsworthy, however, though severe to austerity in his conceptions and nothing if not serious in treatment, certainly puts upon us something of the compelling grip of the true dramatist in such plays as *The Silver Box, Strife* and, strongest of them all and one of the finest examples of modern tragedy, *Justice*, where the themes are so handled as to increase their intrinsic value. This able and high-aiming novelist, when he turns to another technique, takes the trouble to acquire it and becomes a stage influence to reckon with. *The Pigeon*, the most genial outcome of his dramatic art, is a delightful play: and *The Eldest Son, The Fugitive* and *The Mob*, if none of them have been stage successes, stand for work of praiseworthy strength.

On the side of poetry, and coming a little before the Irish drama attracted general attention, Stephen Phillips proved that a poet could learn the technique of the theater and satisfy the demands of reader and play-goer. Saturated with literary traditions, frankly turning to history, legend, and literature itself for his inspiration, Mr. Phillips has written a number of acting dramas, all of them possessing stage value, while remaining real poetry. His best things are *Paolo and Francesca* and *Herod*, the former a play of lovely lyric quality and genuinely dramatic moments of suspense and climax; the latter a powerful handling of the Bible motive. Very fine too in its central character is *Nero*; and *Ulysses*, while less suited to the stage, where it seems spectacle rather than drama, is filled with noble poetry and has a last act that is a little play in itself. Several of Mr. Phillips' best plays have been elaborately staged and successfully produced by representative actor-managers like Sir Herbert Beerbohm Tree and Sir George Alexander.

Still with poetry in mind, it may be added that Lawrence Binyon has given evidence of distinct power in dramatic poetry in his *Attila*, and the delicate Pierrot play, *Prunella*, by Messrs. Housman and Granville Barker is a success in quite another genre.

Israel Zangwill has turned, like Barrie, Galsworthy and Bennett, from fiction to the play, and *The Children of the Ghetto, Merely Mary Ann, The Melting Pot, The War God* and *The Next Religion* show progressively a firmer technique and the use of larger themes. Other playwrights like Alfred Sutro, Sidney Grundy, W. S. Maugham, Hubert Davies, and Captain Marshall have a skillful hand, and in the cases of Maugham and Davies, especially the latter, clever social satire has come from their pens. Louis R. Parker has shown his range and skill in successful dramas so widely divergent as *Rosemary, Pomander Walk* and *Disraeli*.

It may be seen from this category, suggestive rather than complete, that there is in England ample evidence for the statement that drama is now being vigorously produced and must be reckoned with as an appreciable and welcome part of contemporary letters. In the United States, so far, the showing is slighter and less impressive. Yet it is within the facts to say that the native play-making has waxed more serious-minded and skillful (this especially in the last few years) and so has become a definite adjunct to the general movement toward the reinvestiture of drama.

In the prose drama which attempts honestly to reproduce American social conditions, elder men like Howard and Herne, and later ones like Thomas, Gillette and Clyde Fitch, have done worthy pioneer work. Among many younger playwrights who are fast pressing to the front, Eugene Walter, who in *The Easiest Way* wrote one of the best realistic plays of the day, Edward Sheldon, with a dozen interesting dramas to his credit, notably *The Nigger* and *Romance*; and William Vaughan Moody, whose material in both *The Great Divide* and *The Faith Healer* is healthfully American and truthful, although the handling is romantic and that of the poet, deserve first mention.

Women are increasingly prominent in this recent activity and in such hands as those of Rachel Crothers, Ann Flexner, Marguerite Merrington, Margaret Mayo and Eleanor Gates our social life is likely to be exploited in a way to hint at its problems, and truthfully and amusingly set forth its types.

Moody, though he wrote his stage plays in prose, was essentially the poet in viewpoint and imagination. A poet too, despite the fact that more than half his work is in prose, is Percy Mackaye, the son of a distinguished earlier playwright and theater reformer, author of *Hazel Kirke* and *Paul Kauvar*. Mr. Mackaye's prose comedy *Mater*, high comedy in the best sense, and his satiric burlesque, *Anti-Matrimony*, together with the thoughtful drama *Tomorrow*, which seeks to incorporate the new conception of eugenics in a vital story of the day, are good examples of one aspect of his work; and *Jeanne d'Arc, Sapho and Phaon*, verse plays, and the romantic spectacle play, *A Thousand Years Ago*, illustrate his poetic endeavor. Taking a hint from a short story by Hawthorne, he has written in *The Scarecrow* one of the strongest and noblest serious dramas yet wrought by an American. He has also done much for the pageant and outdoor masque, as his *The Canterbury Pilgrims*,

Sanctuary and *St. Louis, A Civic Masque*, presented in May of 1914 on an heroic scale in that city, testify. A poet, whether in lyric or dramatic expression, is Josephine Preston Peabody. Her lovely reshaping of the familiar legend known best in the hands of Browning, *The Piper*, took the prize at the Stratford on Avon spring Shakespeare festival some years ago, and has been successful since both in England and America. Her other dramatic writing has not as yet met so well the stage demands, but is conspicuous for charm and ideality.

In the imaginative field of romance, poetry and allegory we may also place the Americanized Englishman, Charles Rann Kennedy, who has put the touch of the poet and prophet upon homely modern material. His beautiful morality play, *The Servant in the House*, secured his reputation and later plays from *The Winter Feast* to *The Idol Breaker*, inclusive of several shorter pieces, the one act form being definitely practiced by this author, have been interesting work, skillful of technique and surcharged with social sympathy and significance. Edward Knoblauch, the author of *The Faun*, of *Milestones* in collaboration with Mr. Bennett, and of the fantastic oriental divertissement, *Kismet*; and Austin Strong, who wrote *The Toymaker of Nuremberg*, are among the younger dramatists from whom much may yet be expected.

In this enumeration, all too scant to do justice to newer drama in the United States, especially in the field of realistic satire and humorous perception of the large-scaled clashes of our social life, it must be understood that I perforce omit to mention fully two score able and earnest young workers who are showing a most creditable desire to depict American conditions and have learned, or are rapidly learning, the use of their stage tools. The purpose here is to name enough of personal accomplishment to buttress the claim that a promising school has arisen on the native soil with aims and methods similar to those abroad.

And all this work, English or American, shows certain ear-marks to bind it together and declare it of our day in comparison with the past. What are these distinctive features?

On the side of technique, a greater and greater insistence on telling the story dramatically, with more of truth, to the exclusion of all that is non-dramatic, although preserved in the conventions of the theater for perhaps centuries; the elimination of subplot and of subsidiary characters which were of old deemed necessary for purposes of exposition; the avoidance of the prologue and such ancient and useful devices as the aside and the soliloquy; and such simplification of form that the typical play shall reduce itself most likely to three acts, and is almost always less than five; a play that often has but one scene where the action is compressed within the time limits of a few hours, or, at the most, a day or two. All this is the outcome of the influence of Ibsen with its subtlety, expository methods and its intenser psychology. In word, dress, action and scene, too, this modern type of drama approximates closer to life; and inclines to minimize scenery save as congruous background, thus implying a distinct rebellion from the stupidly literal scenic envisagement for which the influence of a Belasco is responsible. The new technique also has, in its seeking for an effect of verisimilitude, adopted the naturalistic key of life in its acting values and has built small theaters better adapted to this quieter, more penetrating presentation.

In regard to subject matter, and the author's attitude to his work, a marked tendency may be seen to emphasize personality in the character drawing, to make it of central interest (contrasted with plot) and a bold attempt to present it in the more minute variations of motive and act rather than in those more obvious reactions to life which have hitherto characterized stage treatment; and equally noticeable if not the dominant note of this latter-day drama, has been the social sympathy expressed in it and making it fairly resonant with kindly human values: the author's desire to see justice done to the under-dog in the social struggle; to extend a fraternal hand to the derelicts of the earth, to understand the poor and strive to help those who are weak or lost; all the underlings and incompetents and ill-doers of earth find their explainers and defenders in these writers. This is the note which sounds in the fraternalism of Kennedy's *The Servant in the House*, the arraignment of society in Walter's *The Easiest Way* and Paterson's *Rebellion*, the contrast of the ideals of east and west in Moody's *The Great Divide*, and the democratic fellowship of Sheldon's *Salvation Nell*. It is the note abroad which gives meaning to Hauptmann's *The Weavers*, Galsworthy's *Justice* and Wedekind's *The Awakening of Spring*, different as they are from each other. It stands for a tolerant, even loving comprehension of the other fellow's case. There is in it a belief in the age, too, and in modern man; a faith in democracy and an aspiration to see established on the earth a social condition which will make democracy a fact, not merely a convenient political catch-word.

Some authors, in their obsession with truth on the stage, have too much neglected the fundamental demands of the theater and so sacrificed the crisp crescendo treatment of crisis in climax as to indulge in a tame, undramatic and bafflingly subtle manipulation of the story; a remark applicable, for example, to a writer like Granville Barker.

But the growth and gains in both countries, with America modestly second, are encouraging. In these modern hands the play has been simplified, deepened, made more truthful, more sympathetic; and is now being given the expressional form that means literature. The bad, the cheap, the flimsy are still being produced, of course, in plenty; so has it always been, so ever will be. But the drama that is worthy, skillful, refreshing in these different kinds—farce, comedy light, polite, or satiric; broad comedy or high, melodrama, tragedy, romance and morality—is now offered, steadily, generously, and it depends upon the theater-goer who has trained himself to know, to reject and accept rightly, to appreciate and so make secure the life of all drama that is worth preservation.

This survey of the English theater and the drama which has been produced in it from the beginning—a survey the brevity of which will not detract, it may be hoped, from its clearness, may serve to place our playgoer in a position the better to appreciate the present conditions; and to give him more respect for a form of literature which he turns to today for intelligent recreation, deeming it a helpfully stimulating form of art. From this vantage-point, he may now approach a consideration of the drama as an artistic problem. He will be readier than before, perhaps, to realize that the playwright, with this history behind him, is the creature of a long and important development, in a double sense: in his treatment of life, and in the manner of that treatment.

Naturally, the theater-goer will not stop with the English product. The necessity alone of understanding Ibsen, as the main figure in this complex modern movement, will lead him to a study of the author of *A Doll's House*. And, working from center to circumference, he will with ever increasing stimulation and delight become familiar with many other foreign dramatists of national or international importance. He will give attention to those other Scandinavians, Strindberg, Drachman and Björnson; to the Russians, Tolstoy, Tchekoff and Gorky; to Frenchmen like Rostand and Maeterlinck, Becque, Hervieu, Lavedan, Donnay and Brieux; to the Germans and Austrians, Hauptmann, Sudermann, Wedekind, Hofmansthal and Schnitzler; to the Italian, D'Annunzio, and the Spanish Echgeragay,—to mention but a few. It may even be that, once aroused to the value of the expression of the Present in these representative writers for the stage, he will wish to trace the dramatic history behind them in their respective countries, as he has (supposedly) already done with the dramatists of his own tongue. If he do so, the play-goer will surely add greatly not only to his general literary culture but to his power of true appreciation of the play of the moment he may be witnessing. For all this reading and reflection and comparison will tend to make him a critic-in-the-seat who settles the fate of plays today because he knows the plays of yesterday and yesteryear.

Chapter 6

The Play as Theme and Personal View

We may now come directly to a consideration of the play regarded as a work of art and a piece of life. After all, this is the central aim in the attempt to become intelligent in our play-going. A play may properly be thought of as a theme; it has a definite subject, which involves a personal opinion about life on the author's part; a view of human beings in their complex interrelations the sum of which make up man's existence on this globe.

The play has a story, of course, and that story is so handled as to constitute a plot: meaning a tangle of circumstances in which the fates of a handful of human beings are involved, a tangle to which it is the business of the plot to give meaning and direction. But back of the story, in any drama that rises to some worth, there is a theme, in a sense. Thus, the theme of *Macbeth* is the degenerating effect of sin upon the natures of the king and his spouse; and the theme of Ibsen's *A Doll's House* is the evil results of treating a grown-up woman as if she were a mere puppet with little or no relation to life's serious realities.

The thing that gives dignity and value to any play is to be found just here: a distinctive theme, which is over and above the interest of story-plot, sinks into the consciousness of the spectator or reader, and gives him stimulating thoughts about life and living long after he may have quite forgotten the fable which made the framework for this suggestive impulse of the dramatist. Give the statement a practical test. Plenty of plays suffice well enough perhaps to fill an evening pleasantly, yet have no theme at all, no idea which one can take with him from the playhouse and ruminate at leisure. For, although the story may be skillfully handled and the technique of the piece be satisfying, if it is not *about* anything, the rational auditor is vaguely dissatisfied and finds in the final estimate that all such plays fall below those that really have a theme. To illustrate: Mr. Augustus Thomas's fine play, *The Witching Hour*, has a theme embedded in a good, old-fashioned melodramatic story; and this is one of the reasons for its great success. But the same author's *Mrs. Leffingwell's Boots*, though executed with practiced skill, has no theme at all and therefore is at the best an empty, if amusing, trifle, far below the dramatist's full powers. Frankly, it is a pot boiler. And, similarly, Mr. Thomas's capital western American drama, *Arizona*, while primarily and apparently story for its own sake, takes on an added virtue because it illustrates, in a story-setting, certain typical and worthy American traits to be found at the time and under those conditions in the far west. To have a theme is not to be didactic, neither to argue for a thesis nor moot a problem. It is simply to have an opinion about life involved in and rising naturally out of the story, and never, never lugged in by the heels. The true dramatist does not tell a story because he has a theme he wishes to impose upon the audience; on the contrary, he tells his story because he sees life that way, in terms of plot, of drama, and in its course, and in spite of himself, a certain notion or view about sublunary things enters into the structure of the whole creation, and emanates from it like an atmosphere. One of the very best comedies of modern times is the late Sidney Grundy's *A Pair of Spectacles*. It has sound technique, delightful characterization, and a simple, plausible, coherent and interesting fable. But, beyond this, it has a theme, a heart-warming one: namely, that one who sees life through the kindly lenses of the optimist is not only happier, but gets the best results from his fellow beings; in short, is nearer the truth. And no one should doubt that this theme goes far toward explaining the remarkable vogue of this admirable comedy. Without a theme so clear, agreeable and interpretive, a play equally skillful would never have had like fortune.

And this theme in a play, as was hinted, must, to be acceptable, express the author's personal opinion, honestly, fearlessly put forth. If it be merely what he ought to think in the premises, what others conventionally think, what it will, in his opinion, or that of the producer of the play, pay to think, the drama will not ring true, and will be likely to fail, even if the technique of a lifetime bolster it up. It must embody a truth relative to the writer, a fact about life as he sees it, and nothing else. A theme in a play cannot be abstract truth, for to tell us of abstract truth is the *métier* of the philosopher, and herein lies his difference from the stage story-teller. Relative truth is the play-maker's aim and the paramount demand upon him is that he be sincere. He must give a view of life in his story which is an honest statement of what human beings and human happenings really are in his experience. If his experience has been so peculiar or unique as to make his themes absurd and impossible to people in general, then his play will pretty surely fail. He pays the penalty of his warped, or too limited or degenerate experience. No matter: show the thing as he sees it and knows it, that he must; and then take his chances.

And so convincing, so winning is sincerity, that even when the view that lies at the heart of the theme appears monstrous and out of all belief, yet it will stand a better chance of acceptance than if the author had trimmed his sails to every wind of favor that blows.

Mr. Kennedy wrote an odd drama a few years ago called *The Servant in the House*, in which he did a most unconventional thing in the way of introducing a mystic stranger out of the East into the midst of an ordinary mundane English household. Anybody examining such a play in advance, and aware of what sort of drama was typical of our day, might have been forgiven had he absolutely refused to have faith in such a work. But the author was one person who did have faith in it; he had a fine theme: the idea that the Christ ideal, when projected into daily life—instead of cried up once a week in church—and there acted on, is efficacious. He had an unshaken belief in this idea. And he conquered, because he dared to substitute for the conventional and supposed inevitable demand an apparently unpopular personal conviction. He found, as men who dare commonly do, that the assumed personal view was the general view which no one had had the courage before to express.

In the same way, M. Maeterlinck, another idealist of the day, wrote *The Blue Bird*. It is safe to say that those in a position to be wise in matters dramatic would never have predicted the enormous success of this simple child play in various countries. But the writer dared to vent his ideas and feelings with regard to childhood and concerning the spiritual aspirations of all mankind; in other words, he chose a theme for some other reason than because it was good, tried theater material; and the world knows the result. It may be said without hesitation that more plays fail in the attempt to modify view in favor of the supposed view of others—the audience, the manager or somebody else—than fail because the dramatist has sturdily stuck to his point of view and honestly set down in his story his own private reaction to the wonderful thing called life; a general possession and yet not one thing, but having as many sides as there are persons in the world to live it.

Consider, for example, the number of dramas that, instead of carrying through the theme consistently to the end, are deflected from their proper course through the playwright's desire (more often it is an unwilling concession to others' desire) to furnish that tradition-condiment, a "pleasant ending." Now everybody normal would rather have a play end well than not; he who courts misery for its own sake is a fool. But, if not a fool, he does not wish the pleasantness at the expense of truth, because then the pleasantness is no longer pleasant to the educated taste, and so defeats its own end. And it is an observed fact that some stories, whether fiction or drama, "begin to end well," as Stevenson expressed it; while others, just as truly, begin to end ill. Hence, when such themes are manhandled by the cheap, dishonest wresting of events or characters or both, so as presumably to send the audience home "happy," we get a wretched malversion of art,—and without at all attaining the object in view. For even the average, or garden-variety, of audience is uneasy at the insult offered its intelligence in such a nefarious transaction. It has been asked to witness a piece of real life, for, testimony to the contrary notwithstanding, that is what an audience takes every play to be. Up to a certain point, this presentation of life is convincing; then, for the sake of leaving an impression that all is well because two persons are united who never should be, or because the hero didn't die when he really did, or because coincidence is piled on coincidence to make a fairy tale situation at which a fairly intelligent cow would rebel, presto, a lie has to be told that would not deceive the very children in the seats. It is pleasant to record truthfully that this miserable and mistaken demand on the part of the short-sighted purveyors of commercialized dramatic wares is yielding gradually to the more enlightened notion that any audience wants a play to be consistent with itself, and feels that too high a price can be paid even for the good ending whose false deification has played havoc with true dramatic interests.

Another mode of dishonesty, in which the writer of a play fails in theme, is to be found whenever, instead of sticking to his subject matter and giving it the unity of his main interest and the wholeness of effect derived from paying it undivided attention, extraneous matter is introduced for the sake of temporary alleviation. Not to stick to your theme is almost as bad at times as to have none. No doubt the temptation comes to all practical playwrights and is a considerable one. But it must be resisted if they are to remain self-respecting artists. The late Clyde Fitch, skilled man of the theater though he was, sinned not seldom in this respect. He sometimes introduced scenes effective for novelty and truth of local color, but so little related to the whole that the trained auditor might well have met him with the famous question asked by the Greek audiences of their dramatists who strayed from their theme: "What has this to do with Apollo?" The remark applies to the drastically powerful scene in his posthumous play *The City*, where the theme which was plainly announced in the first act is lost sight of in the dramatist's desire to use material well adapted to secure a sensational effect in his climax. It is only fair to say that, had this drama received the final molding at the author's hands, it might have been modified to some extent. But there is no question that this was a tendency with Fitch.

The late Oscar Wilde had an almost unparalleled gift for witty epigrammatic dialogue. In his two clever comedies, *Lady Windermere's Fan* and *A Woman of No Importance*, he allowed this gift to run away with him to such an extent that the opening acts of both pieces contain many speeches lifted from his notebooks, seemingly, and placed arbitrarily in the mouths of sundry persons of the play: some of the speeches could quite as well have been spoken by others. This constituted a defect which might have seriously militated against the success of those dramas had they not possessed in full measure brilliant qualities of genuine constructive play-making. The theme, after all, was there, once it was started; and so was the deft handling. But dialogue not motivated by character or necessitated by story is always an injury, and much drama today suffers from this fault. The producer of the play declares that its tone is too steadily serious and demands the insertion of some humor to lighten it, and the playwright, poor, helpless wight, yields, though he knows he is sinning against the Holy Ghost of his art. Or perhaps the play is too short to fill the required time and so padding is deemed necessary—When our theater has become thoroughly artistic, plays will not, as at present, be stretched out beyond the natural size, but will be confined to a shorter playing time and the evening filled out with a curtain raiser or after piece, as is now so common abroad. Or it may be that the ignorance or short-sightedness of those producing the play will lead them to confuse the interests of the chief player with that of the piece itself; and so a departure from theme follows, and unity be sacrificed. That is what unity means: sticking to theme.

And unity of story, be sure, waits on unity of theme. This insistence upon singleness of purpose in a play, clinging to it against all allurements, does not imply that what is known as a subplot may not be allowed in a drama. It was common in the past and can still be seen today, though the tendency of modern technique is to abandon it for the sake of greater emphasis upon the main plot and the resulting tightening of the texture, avoiding any risk of a splitting of interest. However, a secondary or subplot in the right hands—as we see it in Shakespeare's *Merchant of Venice*, or, for a modern instance, in Pinero's *Sweet Lavender*—is legitimate enough. Those who manipulate it with success will be careful to see that the minor plot shall never appear for a moment to be major; and that both strands shall be interwoven into an essential unity of design, which is admirably illustrated in Shakespeare's comedy just mentioned.

Have a theme then, let it be quite your own, and stick to it, is a succinct injunction which every dramatist will do well to heed and the critic in the seat will do well to demand. Neither one nor the other should ever forget that the one and only fundamental unity in drama, past, present and to come, is unity of idea, and the unity of action which gathers about that idea as surely as iron filings around the magnetized center. The unities of time and place are conditional upon the kind of drama aimed at, and the temporal and physical characteristic of the theater; the Greeks obeyed them for reasons peculiar to the Greeks, and many lands, beginning with the Romans, have imitated these so-called laws since. But Shakespeare destroyed them for England, and today, if unity of time and place are to be seen in an Ibsen play, it simply means that, in the psychological drama he writes, time and place are naturally restricted. But in the unity of action which means unity of theme we have a principle which looks to the constitution of the human mind; for the sake of that ease of attention which helps to hold interest and produce pleasure, such unity there must be; the mind of man (when he has one) is made that way.

There is a special reason why the intelligent playgoer must insist upon this fundamental unity: because much in our present imaginative literature is, as to form, in direct conflict with that appeal to a sustained effect of unity offered by a well-wrought drama. The short story that is all too brief, the vaudeville turn, the magazine habit of reading a host of unrelated scamped trifles, all militate against the habit of concentrated attention; all the more reason why it should be cultivated.

Let me return to the thought that the dramatist, in making the theme his own, may be tempted to present a view of life not only personal but eccentric and vagarious to the point of insanity.

His view, to put it bluntly, may represent a crackbrained distortion of life rather than life as it is experienced by men in general. In such a case, and obviously, his drama will be ineffective and objectionable, in the exact degree that it departs from what may be called broadly the normal and the possible. As I have already asserted, distortion for distortion, even a crazy handling of theme that is honest is to be preferred to one consciously a deflection from belief. But the former is not right because the latter is wrong. Both should be avoided, and will be if the play-maker be at the same time sincere and healthily representative in his reaction to life of humanity at large. The really great plays, and the good plays that have shown a lasting quality, have sinned in neither of these particulars.

It is especially of import that our critic-in-the-seat should insist on this matter of normal appeal, because ours happens to be a day when personal vagaries, extravagant theories and lawless imaginings are granted a freedom in literary and other art in general such as an earlier day hardly conceived of. The abuses under the mighty name of Art are many and flagrant. All the more need for the knowing spectator in the theater, or he who reads the play at home, to be prepared for his function, quick to reprimand alike tame subserviency or the abnormalities of unrestrained "genius." It is fair to say that absolute honesty on the dramatist's part in the conception and presentation of theme will meet all legitimate criticisms of his work. Within his limitations, we shall get the best that is in him, if he will only show us life as he sees it, and have the courage of his convictions, allowing no son of man to warp his work from that purpose.

Chapter 7

Method and Structure

I

So far we have considered the material of the dramatist, his theme and subject matter, and his attitude toward it. But his method in conceiving this material and of handling it is of great importance and we may now examine this a little in detail, to realize the peculiar problem that confronts him.

At the beginning let it be understood that the dramatist must see his subject dramatically. Every stage story should be seen or conceived in a central moment which is the explanation of the whole play, its reason for being. Without that moment, the drama could not exist; if the story were told, the plot unfolded without presenting that scene, the play would fall flat, nay, there would, strictly speaking, be no play there. That is why the French (leaders in nomenclature, as in all else dramatic) call it the *scène à faire*, the scene that one must do; or, to adopt the English equivalent offered by Mr. Archer in his interesting and able manual of stagecraft entitled *Playmaking*, the obligatory scene: that is, the scene one is obliged to show. This moment in the story is a climax, because it is the crowning result of all the preceding growth of the drama up to a point where the steadily increasing interest has reached its height and an electric effect of suspense and excitement results. This suspensive excitement depends upon the clash of human wills against each other or against circumstances; events are so tangled that they can be no further involved and something must happen in the way of cutting the knot; the fates of the persons are so implicated that their lives must be either saved or destroyed, in order to break the deadlock. Thus along with the clash goes a crisis presented in a breathless climactic effect which is the central and imperative scene of the piece, the backbone of every good play.

If this obligatory scene be absent, you may at once suspect the dramatist; whatever his other virtues (fine dialogue, excellent characterization, or still other merits), it is probable he is not one genuinely called to tell a story in the manner of drama within stage limitations.

It is sometimes said that a play is written backward. The remark has in mind this fundamental fact of the climax; all that goes before leads up to it, is preparation for it, and might conceivably be written after the obligatory scene has been conceived and shaped; all that comes after it is an attempt to retire gracefully from the great moment, rounding it out, showing its results, and conducting the spectator back to the common light of day in such a way as not to be dull, or conventional or anti-climactic. What follows this inevitable scene is (however disguised) at bottom a sort of bridge conveying the auditor from the supreme pleasure of the theater back to the rather humdrum experience of actual life; it is an experiment in gradation. And the prepared playgoer will deny the coveted award of *well done* to any play, albeit from famous hands and by no means wanting in good qualities, which nevertheless fails in this prime requisite of good drama: the central, dynamic scene illuminating all that goes before and follows after, without which the play, after all, has no right to existence.

With the coming of the modern psychologic school of which Galsworthy, Barker and Bennett are exemplars, there is a distinct tendency to minimize or even to eliminate this obligatory scene; an effort which should be carefully watched and remonstrated against; since it is the laying of an axe at the roots of dramatic writing.

It may be confessed that in some instances the results of this violation of a cardinal principle are so charming as to blind the onlooker perhaps to the danger; as in the case of *Milestones* by Messrs. Bennett and Knoblauch, or *The Pigeon* by Galsworthy, or Louis Parker's Georgian picture, *Pomander Walk*. But this only confuses the issue. Such drama may prove delightful for other reasons; the thing to bear in mind is that they are such in spite of the giving up of the peculiar, quintessential merit of drama in its full sense. Their virtues are non-dramatic virtues, and they succeed, in so far as success awaits them, in spite of the violation of a principle, not because of it. They can be, and should be, heartily enjoyed, so long as this is plainly understood and the two accomplishments are perceived as separate. For it may be readily granted that a pleasant and profitable evening at the theater may be spent, without the very particular appeal which is dramatic coming into the experience at all. There are more things in the modern theater than drama; which is well, if we but make the discrimination.

But for the purposes of intelligent comprehension of what is drama, just that and naught else, the theater-goer will find it not amiss to hold fast to the idea that a play without its central scene hereinbefore described is not a play in the exact definition of that form of art, albeit ever so enjoyable entertainment. The history of drama in its failures and successes bears out the statement. And of all nations, France can be studied most profitably with this in mind, since the French have always been past masters in the feeling for the essentially dramatic, and centuries ago developed the skill to produce it. The fact that we get such a term as the *scène à faire* from them points to this truth.

Accepting the fact, then, that a play sound in conception and construction has and must have a central scene which acts as a centripetal force upon the whole drama, unifying and solidifying it, the next matter to consider is the subdivision of the play into acts and scenes. Since the whole story is shown before the footlights, scenes and acts are such divisions as shall best mark off and properly accentuate the stages of the story, as it is unfolded. Convention has had something to do with this arrangement and number, as we learn from a glance at the development of the stage story. The earlier English drama accepted the five-act division under classic influence, though the greatest dramatist of the past, Shakespeare, did so only half-heartedly, as may be realized by looking at the first complete edition of his plays, the First Folio of 1621. *Hamlet*, for instance, as there printed, gives the first two acts, and thereafter is innocent of any act division; and *Romeo and Juliet* has no such division at all. But with later editors, the classic tradition became more and more a convention and the student with the modernized text in hand has no reason to suspect the original facts. An old-fashioned work like Freitag's *Technique of the Drama* assumes this form as final and endeavors to study dramatic construction on that assumption.

The scenes, too, were many in the Elizabethan period, for the reason that there was no scene shifting in the modern sense; as many scenes might therefore be imagined as were desirable during the continuous performance. It has remained for modern technique to discover that there was nothing irrevocable about this fivefold division of acts; and that, in the attempt at a general simplification of play structure, we can do better by a reduction of them to three or four. Hence, five acts have shrunk to four or three; so that today the form preferred by the best dramatic artists, looking to Ibsen for leadership, is the three-act play, though the nature of the story often makes four desirable. A careful examination of the best plays within a decade will serve to show that this is definitely the tendency.

The three-act play, with its recognition that every art structure should have a beginning, middle and end—

Aristotle's simple but profound observation on the tragedy of his day—might seem to be that which marks the ultimate technique of drama; yet it would be pedantic and foolish to deny that the simplification may proceed further still and two acts succeed three, or, further still, one act embrace the complete drama, thus returning to the "scene individable" of the Greeks and Shakespeare. Certainly, the whole evolution of form points that way.

But, whatever the final simplification, the play as a whole will present certain constructive problems; problems which confront the aim ever to secure, most economically and effectively, the desired dramatic result. The first of these is the problem of the opening act, which we may now examine in particular.

II

The first act has a definite aim and difficulties that belong to itself alone. Broadly speaking, its business is so to open the story as to leave the audience at the fall of the first curtain with a clear idea of what it is about; not knowing too much, wishing to know more, and having well in mind the antecedent conditions which made the story at its beginning possible. If, at the act's end, too much has been revealed, the interest projected forward sags; if too little, the audience fails to get the idea around which the story revolves, and so is not pleasurably anxious for its continuance. If the antecedent conditions have not clearly been made manifest, some omitted link may throw confusion upon all that follows. On the other hand, if too much time has been expended in setting forth the events that lead up to the story's start on the stage, with the rise of the curtain, not enough time may be left, within act limits, to hold the attention and fix interest so it may sustain the entr'act break and fasten upon the next act.

Thus it will be seen that a successful opening act is a considerable test of the dramatist's skill.

Another drawback complicates the matter. The playwright has at his disposal in the first act from half to three-quarters of an hour in which to effect his purpose. But he must lose from five to ten minutes of this precious time allotment, at the best very short, because, according to the detestable Anglo-Saxon convention, the audience is not fairly seated when the play begins, and general attention therefore not riveted upon the stage action. Under ideal conditions, and they have never existed in all respects in any time or country, the audience will be in place at the curtain's rise, alert to catch every word and movement. As a matter of fact, this practically never occurs; particularly in America, where the drama has never been taken so seriously as an art as music; for some time now people have not been allowed, in a hall devoted to that gentle sister art, to straggle in during the performance of a composition, or the self-exploitation of a singer, thereby disturbing the more enlightened hearers who have come on time, and regard it, very properly, as part of their breeding to do so. But in the theater, as we all know, the barbarous custom obtains of admitting late comers, so that for the first few minutes of the performance a steady insult is thus offered to the play, the players, and the portion of the audience already in their seats. It may be hoped, parenthetically, that as our theater gradually becomes civilized this survival of the manners of bushmen may become purely historic. At present, however, the practical playwright accepts the existing conditions, as perforce he must, and writes his play accordingly. And so the first few minutes of a well-constructed drama, it may be noticed, are generally devoted to some incident, interesting or amusing in itself, preferably external so as to catch the eye, but not too vital, and involving, as a rule, minor characters, without revealing anything really crucial in the action. The matter presented thus is not so much important as action that leads up to what is important; and its lack of importance must not be implied in too barefaced a way, lest attention be drawn to it. This part of the play marks time, and yet is by way of preparation for the entrance of the main character or characters.

Much skill is needed, and has been developed, in regard to the marshaling of the precedent conditions: to which the word *exposition* has been by common consent given. Exposition today is by no means what it was in Shakespeare's; indeed, it has been greatly refined and improved upon. In the earlier technique this prefatory material was introduced more frankly and openly in the shape of a prologue; or if the prologue was not used, at least the information was conveyed directly and at once to the audience by means of minor characters, stock figures like the servant or confidante, often employed mainly, or even solely, for that purpose. This made the device too obvious for modern taste, and such as to injure the illusion; the play lost its effect of presenting truthfully a piece of life, just when it was particularly important to seem such; that is, at the beginning. For with the coming of the subtler methods culminating in the deft technique of an Ibsen, which aims to draw ever closer to a real presentation of life on the stage, and so strove to find methods of depiction which should not obtrude artifice except when unavoidable, the stage artist has learned to interweave these antecedent circumstances with the story shown on the stage before the audience. And the result is that today the exposition of an Ibsen, a Shaw, a Wilde, a Pinero or a Jones is so managed as hardly to be detected save by the expert in stage mechanics. The intelligent play-goer will derive pleasure and profit from a study of Ibsen's growth in this respect; observing, for example, how much more deftly exposition is hidden in a late work like *Hedda Gabler* than in a comparatively early one like *Pillars of Society*; and, again, how bald and obvious was this master's technique in this respect when he began in the middle of the nineteenth century to write his historical plays.

In general, it is well worth while to watch the handling of the first act on the part of acknowledged craftsmen with respect to the important matter of introducing into the framework of a two hours' spectacle all that has transpired before the picture is exhibited to the spectators.

One of the definite dangers of the first act is that of giving an audience a false lead as to character or turn of story. By some bit of dialogue, or even by an interpolated gesture on the part of an actor who transcends his rights (a misleading thing, as likely as not to be charged to the playwright), the auditor is put on a wrong scent, or there is aroused in him an expectation never to be realized. Thus the real issue is obscured, and later trouble follows as the true meaning is divulged. A French critic, commenting on the performance in Paris of a play by Bernard Shaw, says that its meaning was greatly confused because two of the characters took the unwarranted liberty of exchanging a kiss, for which, of course, there was no justification in the stage business as indicated by the author. All who know Shaw know that he has very little interest in stage kisses.

Closely associated with this mistake, and far more disastrous, is such a treatment of act one as to suggest a theme full of interest and therefore welcome, which is then not carried through the remainder of the drama. Fitch's *The City* has been already referred to with this in mind. A more recent example may be found in Veiller's popular melodrama, *Within the Law*. The extraordinary vogue of this melodrama is sufficient proof that it possesses some of the main qualities of skillful theater craft: a strong, interesting fable, vital characterization, and considerable feeling for stage situation and climax, with the forthright hand of execution. Nevertheless, it distinctly fails to keep the promise of the first act, where, at the fall of the curtain, the audience has become particularly interested in a sociological problem, only to be asked in the succeeding acts to forget it in favor of a conventional treatment of stock melodramatic material, with the usual thieves, detectives pitted against each other, and gunplay for the central scene of surprise and capture. That such current plays as *The City* and *Within the Law* can get an unusual hearing, in spite of these defects, suggests the uncritical nature of American audiences; but quite as truly implies that drama may be very good, indeed, in most respects while falling short of the caliber we demand of masterpieces.

With the opening act, then, so handled as to avoid these pitfalls, the dramatist is ready to go on with his task. He has sufficiently aroused the interest of his audience to give it a pleasurable sense of entertainment ahead, without imparting so much knowledge as to leave too little for guesswork and lessen the curiosity necessary for one who must still spend an hour and a half in a place of bad air and too heated temperature. He has awakened attention and directed it upon a theme and story, yet left it tantalizingly but not confusingly incomplete. Now he has before him the problem of unfolding his play and making it center in the climactic scene which will make or mar the piece. We must observe, then, how he develops his story in that part of the play intermediate between the introduction and the crisis; the second act of a three-act drama or the third if the four-act form be chosen.

Chapter 8

Development

The story being properly started, it becomes the dramatist's business, as we saw, so to advance it that it will develop naturally and with such increase of interest as to tighten the hold upon the audience as the plot reaches its crucial point, the obligatory scene. This can only be done by the sternest selection of those elements of story which can be fitly shown on the stage, or without a loss of interest be inferred clearly from off-stage occurrences. Since action is of the essence of drama, all narrative must be shunned that deals with matters which, being vital to the play and naturally dramatic material, can be presented directly to the eye and ear. And character must be economically handled, so that as it is revealed the revelation at the same time furthers the story, pushing it forward instead of holding it static while the character is being unfolded. Dialogue should always do one of these two things and the best dialogue will do both: develop plot in the very moment that it exhibits the unfolding psychology of the *dramatis personæ*. The fact that in the best modern work plot is for the sake of character rather than the reverse does not violate this principle; it simply redistributes emphasis. Character without plot may possibly be attractive in the hands of a Galsworthy or Barker; but the result is extremely likely to be tame and inconclusive. And, contrariwise, plot without character, that is, with character that lacks individuality and meaning and merely offers a peg upon which to hang a series of happenings, results in primitive drama that, being destitute of psychology, falls short of the finest and most serious possibilities of the stage.

This portion of the play, then, intermediate between introduction and climax, is very important and tries the dramatist's soul, in a way, quite as truly as do beginning and end.

In a three-act play—which we may assume as normal, without forgetting that four are often necessary to the best telling of the story, and that five acts are still found convenient under certain circumstances, as in Rostand's *Cyrano de Bergerac* and Shaw's *Pygmalion*—the work of development falls on the second act, in the main. The climax of action is likely to be at the end of the act, although plays can be mentioned, and good ones, where the playwright has seen fit to place his crucial scene well on into act three. In this matter he is between two dangers and must steer his course wisely to avoid the rocks of his Scylla and Charybdis. If his climax come too soon, an effect of anti-climax is likely to be made, in an act too long when the main stress is over. If, on the other hand, he put his strongest effect at the end of the piece or close to it, while the result is admirable in sustaining interest and saving the best for the last, the close is apt to be too abrupt and unfinished for the purposes of art; sending the audience out into the street, dazed after the shock of the obligatory scene.

Therefore, the skillful playwright inclines to leave sufficient of the play after the climax to make an agreeable rounding out of the fable, tie up loose ends and secure an artistic effect of completing the whole structure without tedium or anti-climax. He thus preserves unity, yet escapes an impression of loose texture in the concluding part of his play. It may be seen that this makes the final act a very special problem in itself, a fact we shall consider in the later treatment.

And now, with the second-act portion of the play in mind, standing for growth, increased tension, and an ever-greater interest, a peculiarity of the play which differentiates it from the fiction-story can be mentioned. It refers to the nature of the interest and the attitude of the auditor toward the story.

In fiction, interest depends largely upon suspense due to the uncertainty of the happenings; the reader, unaware of the outcome of events, has a pleasing sense of curiosity and a stimulating desire to know the end. He reads on, under the prick of this desire. The novelist keeps him more or less in the dark, and in so doing fans the flame of interest. What will be the fate of the hero? Will the heroine escape from the impending doom? Will the two be mated before the Finis is written? Such are the natural questions in a good novel, in spite of all our modern overlaying of fiction with subtler psychologic suggestions.

But the stage story is different. The audience from the start is taken into the dramatist's confidence; it is allowed to know something that is not known to the *dramatis personæ* themselves; or, at least, not known to certain very important persons of the story, let us say, the hero and heroine, to give them the simple old-fashioned description. And the audience, taken in this flattering way into the playwright's secret, finds its particular pleasure in seeing how the blind puppets up on the stage act in an ignorance which if shared by the spectators would qualify, if not destroy, the special kind of excitement they are enjoying.

Just why this difference between play and novel exists is a nice question not so easily answered; that it does exist, nobody who has thought upon the subject can doubt. Occasionally, it is true, successful plays are written in apparent violation of this principle. That eminently skillful and effective piece of theater work, Bernstein's *The Thief*, is an example; a large part of the whole first act, if not all of it, takes place without the spectator suspecting that the young wife, who is the real thief, is implicated in the crime. Nevertheless, such dramas are the exception. Broadly speaking, sound dramaturgy makes use of the principle of knowing cooperation of the audience in the plot, and always will; if for no other reason, because the direct stage method of showing a story makes it impracticable to hoodwink those in the auditorium and also perhaps because the necessary compression of events in a play would make the suddenness of the discovery on the part of the audience that they had been fooled unpleasant: an unpleasantness, it may be surmised, intensified by the additional fact that the fooling has been done in the presence of others—their fellow theater-goers. The quickness of the effects possible to the stage and inability of the playwright to use repetition no doubt also enter in the result. The novelist can return, explain, dwell upon the causes of the reader's readjustment to changed characters or surprising turns of circumstance; the dramatist must go forthright on and make his strokes tell for once and for all.

Be this as it may, the theater story, as a rule, by a tradition which in all probability roots in an instinct and a necessity, invites the listener to be a sort of eavesdropper, to come into a secret and from this vantage point watch the perturbations of a group of less-knowing creatures shown behind the footlights: he not only sees, but oversees. As an outcome of this trait, results follow which also set the play in contrast with the other ways of story telling. The playwright should not deceive his audience either in the manipulation of characters or occurrences. Pleasurable as this may be in fiction, in the theater it is disastrous. The audience, disturbed in its superior sense of knowledge, sitting as it were like the gods apart and asked suddenly, peremptorily, to reconstruct its suppositions, is baffled and then irritated. This is one of several reasons why, in the delineation of character on the stage, it is of very dubious desirability to spring a surprise; making the seeming hero turn out a villain or the presumptive villain blossom into a paragon of all the virtues: as Dickens does in *Our Mutual Friend*; in that case, to the added zest of the reader. The risk in subtilizing stage character lies just here. Persons shown so fleetingly in a few selected moments of their whole lives, after the stage fashion, must be seen in high relief, if they are to be clearly grasped by the onlookers. Conceding that in actual life folk in general are an indeterminate gray rather than stark black and white, it is none the less necessary to use primary colors, for the most part, in painting them, in order that they may be realized. Here again we encounter the limitations of art in depicting life, and its difference therefrom. In a certain sense, therefore, stage characters must be more primitive, more elemental, as well as elementary, than the characters in novels, a thought we shall have occasion to come back to, from another angle, later on.

Equally is it true that good technique forbids the false lead: any hint or suggestion which has the appearance of conducting on to something to come later in the play, which shall verify and fortify the previous allusion or implication. Every word spoken is thus, besides its immediate significance, a preparation for something ahead. It is a continual temptation to a dramatist with a feeling for character (a gift most admirable in itself) to do brushwork on some person of his play, which, while it may illuminate the character as such, may involve episodic treatment that will entirely mislead an audience into supposing that the author has far more meaning in the action shown than he intended. These false leads are of course always the enemies of unity and to be all the more carefully guarded against in proportion to their attraction. So attractive, indeed, is this lure into by-paths away from the main path of progress that it is fairly astonishing to see how often even veteran playwrights fall in love with some character, disproportionately handle it, and invent unnecessary tangential incidents in order to exhibit it. And, rather discouragingly, an audience forgives episodic treatment and over-emphasis in the enjoyment of the character, as such; willing to let the drama suffer for the sake of a welcome detail.

In developing his story in this intermediate part of

it, a more insidious, all-pervasive lure is to be seen in the change in the very type of drama intended at first, or clearly promised in act one. The play may start out to be a comedy of character and then be deflected into one where character is lost sight of in the interest of plot; or a play farcical in the conditions given may turn serious on the dramatist's hands. Or, worse yet, that which is a comedy in feeling and drift, may in the course of the development become tragic in conclusion. Or, once more, what begins for tragedy, with its implied seriousness of interest in character and philosophy of life, may resolve itself, under the fascination of plot and of histrionic effectivism, into melodrama, with its undue emphasis upon external sensation and its correlative loss in depth and artistry.

All these and still other permutations a play suffers in the sin committed whenever the real type or genre of a drama, implied at the start, is violated in the later handling. The history of the stage offers many illustrations. In a play not far, everything considered, from being the greatest in the tongue, Shakespeare's *Hamlet*, it may be questioned if there be not a departure in the final act from the emphasis placed upon psychology in the acts that lead up to it. The character of the melancholy prince is the main thing, the pivot of interest, up to that point; but in the fifth act the external method of completing the story, which involves the elimination of so many of the persons of the play, has somewhat the effect of a change of kind, an abrupt and incongruous cutting of the Gordian knot. Doubtless, the facts as to the composite nature of this play viewed in its total history may have much to do with such an effect, if it be set down here aright. In any case, it is certain that every week during the dramatic season in New York new plays are to be seen which, by this mingling of genres, fall short of the symmetry of true art.

One other requirement in the handling of the play in the section between introduction and climax: the playwright must not linger too long over it, nor yet shorten it in his eagerness to reach the scene which is the crown and culmination of all his labors. Probably the experienced craftsman is likely to make the second mistake rather than the first, though both are often to be noted. He fails sometimes to realize the increase in what I may call reverberatory power which is gained by a slower approach to the great moment through a series of deft suggestions of what is to come; appetizing hints and withdrawals, reconnaitres before the actual engagement, all of it preparatory to the real struggle that is pending. It is a law of the theater, applying to dialogue, character and scene, that twice-told is always an advantage. One distinguished playwright rather cynically declared that you must tell an audience you are going to do it, are doing it, and have done it. Examples in every aspect of theater work abound. The catch phrase put in the mouth of the comic character is only mildly amusing at first; it gains steadily with repetition until, introduced at just the right moment, the house rocks with laughter. Often the difference between a detached witticism, like one of Oscar Wilde's *mots*, and a bit of genuine dramatic humor rests in the fact that the fun lies in the setting: it is a *mot de situation*, to borrow the French expression, not a mere *mot d'esprit*. By appearing to be near a crisis, and then introducing a barrier from which it is necessary to draw back and approach once more over the same ground, tension is increased and tenfold the effect secured when at last the match is laid to the fire.

Plenty of plays fail of their full effect because the climax is come at before every ounce of value has been wrung out of preceding events. If the screen scene in *The School for Scandal* be studied with this principle in mind, the student will have as good an object lesson as English drama can show of skilled leading up to a climax by so many little steps of carefully calculated effect that the final fall of the screen remains one of the great moments in the theater, despite the mundane nature of the theme and the limited appeal to the deeper qualities of human nature. Within its limitations (and theater art, as any other, is to be judged by success under accepted conditions) Sheridan's work in this place and play is a permanent master-stroke of brilliant technique, as well as one explanation of the persistence of that delightful eighteenth century comedy.

But the dramatist, as I have said, may also err in delaying so long in his preparation and growth, that the audience, being ready for the climax before it arrives, will be cold when it comes, and so the effect will hang fire. It is safe to say that in a three-act play, where the first act has consumed thirty-five to forty minutes, and the climax is to occur at the fall of the second curtain, it is well if the intermediate act does not last much above the same length of time. Of course, the nature of the story and the demands it makes will modify the statement; but it applies broadly to the observed phenomena. The first act, for reasons already explained, is apt to be the longest of the three, as the last act is the shortest, other things being equal. If the first act, therefore, run fifty minutes, forty to forty-five, or even thirty-five, would be shapely for act two; which, with twenty to twenty-five minutes given to the final act, would allot to the entire play about two hours and ten minutes, which is close to an ideal playing time for a drama under modern conditions. This time allowance, with the added fraction of minutes given to the entr'acts thrown in, would, for a play which began at 8:15, drop the final curtain at about 10:30.

In case the climax, as has been assumed of a three-act play, be placed at the end of the second act, the third act will obviously be shorter. Should, however, the growth be projected into the third act, and the climax be sprung at a point within this act—beyond the middle, let us say—then the final act is lengthened and act two shortened in proportion. The principle is that, with the main interest over, it is hard to hold the auditor's attention; whereas if the best card is still up the sleeve we may assume willingness to prolong the game.

With the shift of climax from an earlier to a later place in the piece, the technique of the handling is changed only according to these commonsense demands. A knowledge of the psychology of human beings brought together for the purpose of entertainment will go far toward settling the question. And whether the playwright place his culminating effect in act two or three, or whether for good and sufficient reasons of story complication the three acts become four or even five, the principles set forth in the above pages apply with only such modifications as are made necessary by the change.

The theater-goer, seeking to pass an intelligent opinion upon a drama as a whole, will during this period of growth ask of the playwright that he keep the auditor's interest and increase it symmetrically; that he show the plot unfolding in action, instead of talking about it; that he do not reach the eagerly expected conflagration too soon, nor delay it too long; and that he make more and more apparent the meaning of the characters in their relations to each other and to the plot. If the spectator be confused, baffled, irritated or bored, or any or all of these, he has a legitimate complaint against the dramatist. And be it noted that while the majority of a theater audience may not with self-conscious analysis know why they are dissatisfied, under these conditions, the dissatisfaction is there, just the same, and thus do they become critics, though they know it not, even as M. Jourdain talked prose all his days without being aware of it.

Chapter 9

Climax

With the play properly introduced in act one, and the development carried forward upon that firm foundation in the following act or acts, the playwright approaches that part of his play which will, more than anything else, settle the fate of his work. As we have noted, if he have no such scene, he will not have a play at all. If on arrival it fail to seem indispensable and to be of dynamic quality, the play will be broken-winged, at best. The proof that he is a genuine playwright by rightful calling and not a literary person, producing books for closet reading, lies just here. The moment has come when, with his complication brought to the point where it must be solved, and all that has gone before waiting upon that solution, he must produce an effect with one skillful right-arm stroke which shall make the spectators a unit in the feeling that the evening has been well spent and his drama is true to the best tradition of the stage.

The stress has steadily increased to a degree at which it must be relieved. The strain is at the breaking point. The clash of characters or of circumstances operating upon characters is such that a crisis is at hand. By some ingenious interplay of word, action and scene, by an emotional crescendo crystallizing in a stage picture, by some unexpected reversion of incident or of human psychology (known in stage technique as peripety) or by an unforeseen accident in the fall of events, an electric change is exhibited, with the emotions of the *dramatis personæ* at white heat and the consequent enthraldom of the audience. Of all the varied pleasures of the playhouse, this moment, scene, turn of story, is that which appeals to the largest number and has made the theater most distinctive. This is not to say that a profound revelation of character, or a pungent reflection on life, made concrete in a situation, may not be a finer thing to do. It is merely to recognize a certain unique thing the stage can do in story telling, as against other forms, and to confess its universal attraction. While there is much in latter day play-making that seems to deaden the thrill of the obligatory scene, a clear comprehension of its central importance is basal in appreciation of the drama. A play may succeed without it, and a temporary school of psychologues may even pretend to pooh-pooh it as an outworn mode of cheap theatrics. The influence of Ibsen, and there is none more potent, has been cited as against the *scène à faire*, in the French sense; and it is true that his curtains are less obviously stressed and appear to aim not so much at the palpably heightened effects traditional of the development in French hands,—the most skillful hands in the world. But it remains true that this central and dominant scene is inherent in the very structure of dramatic writing. To repeat what was said before, the play that abandons climax may be good entertainment, but is by so much poorer drama. The best and most successful dramaturgy of our day therefore will seek to preserve the obligatory scene, but hide under more subtle technique the ways and means by which it is secured. The ways of the past became so open in the attempt to reach the result as to produce in many cases a feeling of bald artifice. This the later technique will do all in its power to avoid, while clinging persistently to the principle of climax, a principle of life just as truly as a principle of art. Physicians speak in a physiological sense of the grand climacteric of a man's age.

A test of any play may be found in the readiness with which it lends itself to a simple threefold statement of its story; the proposition, as it is called by technicians. This tabloid summary of the essence of the play is valuable in that it reveals plainly two things: whether there is a play in hand, and what and where is its obligatory scene. All who wish to train themselves to be critical rather than captious or silly in their estimate of drama, cannot be too strongly urged to practice this exercise of reducing a play to its lowest terms, its essential elements. It will serve to clarify much that might remain otherwise a muddle. And one of the sure tests of a good play may be found here; if it is not a workable drama, either it will not readily reduce to a proposition or else cannot be stated propositionally at all. Further, a play that is a real play in substance, and not a hopelessly undramatic piece of writing arbitrarily cut up into scenes or acts, and expressed in dialogue (like some of the dramas of the Bengalese Tagore), can be stated clearly and simply in a brief paragraph. This matter of reduction to a skeleton which is structurally a *sine qua non* may be illustrated.

A proposition, to define it a little more carefully, is a threefold statement of the essence of a play, so organically related that each successive part depends upon and issues from the other. It contains a condition (or situation), an action, and a result. For instance, the proposition of *Macbeth* may be expressed as follows:

I. A man, ambitious to be king, abetted by his wife, gains the throne through murder.
II. Remorse visits them both.
III. What will be the effect upon the pair?

Reflection upon this schematic summary will show that the interest of Shakespeare's great drama is not primarily a story interest; plot is not the chief thing, but character. The essential crux lies in the painful spectacle of the moral degeneration of husband and wife, sin working upon each according to their contrasted natures. Both have too much of the nobler elements in them not to experience regret and the prick of conscience. This makes the drama called *Macbeth* a fine example of psychologic tragedy in the true sense.

Or take a well-known modern play, *Camille*:

I. A young man loves and lives with a member of the demi-monde.
II. His father pleads with her to give him up, for his own sake.
III. What will she do?

It will be observed that the way the lady of the camellias answers the question is the revelation of her character; so that the play again, although its story interest is sufficient, is primarily a character study, surrounded by Dumas fils with a rich atmosphere of understanding sympathy and with sentiment that to a later taste becomes sentimentality.

The School for Scandal might be stated in this way:

I. An old husband brings his gay but well-meaning wife to town.
II. Her innocent love of fun involves her in scandal.
III. Will the two be reconciled, and how?

Ibsen's *A Doll's House* may be thus expressed in a proposition:

I. A young wife has been babified by her husband.
II. Experiences open her eyes to the fact that she is not educated to be either wife or mother.
III. She leaves her husband until he can see what a woman should be in the home: a human being, not a doll.

These examples will serve to show what is meant by proposition and indicate more definitely the central purpose of the dramatic author and the technical demand made upon him. Be assured that under whatever varied garb of attraction in incident, scene and character, this underlying stern architectural necessity abides, and a drama's inability to reduce itself thus to a formula is a confession that in the structural sense the building is lop-sided and insecure, or, worse, that there is no structure there at all: nothing, so to put it, but a front elevation, a mere architect's suggestion.

As the spectator breathlessly enjoys the climax and watches to see that unknotting of the knot which gives the French word *dénouement* (unknotting) its meaning, he will notice that the intensity of the climactic effect is not derived alone from action and word; but that largely effective in the total result is the picture made upon the stage, in front of the background of setting which in itself has pictorial quality, by the grouped characters as the curtain falls.

This effect, conventionally called a *situation*, is for the eye as well as for the ear and the brain,—better, the heart. It would be an unfortunate limitation to our theater culture if we did not comprehend to the full how large a part of the effect of a good play is due to the ever-changing series of artistic stage pictures furnished by the dramatist in collaboration with the actors and the stage manager. This principle is important throughout a play, but gets its most vivid illustration in the climax; hence, I enlarge upon it at this point.

Among the most novel, fruitful and interesting experiments now being made in the theater here and abroad may be mentioned the attempts to introduce more subtle and imaginative treatment of the possibilities of color and form in stage setting than have hitherto obtained. The reaction influenced by familiarity with the unadorned simplicity of the Elizabethans, the Gordon Craig symbolism, the frank attempt to substitute artistic suggestion for the stupid and expensive reproduction on the stage of what is called "real life," are phases of this movement, in which Germany and Russia have been prominent. The stage manager and scene deviser are daily becoming more important factors in the production of a play; and along with this goes a clearer perception of the values of grouping and regrouping on the part of the plastic elements behind the footlights. Gordon Craig's book on *The Art of The Theatre* may be consulted for further light upon a movement that is very significant and likely to be far-reaching in time, in its influence upon future stage and dramatic conditions.

Many a scenic moment, many a climax, may be materially damaged by a failure to place the characters in such relative positions as shall visualize the dramatic feeling of the scene and reveal in terms of picture the dramatist's meaning. After all, the time-honored convention that the main character, or characters, should, at the moment when they are dominant in the story, take the center of the stage, is no empty convention; it is based on logic and geometry. There is a direct correspondence between the unity of emotion concentrated in a group of persons and the eye effect which reports that fact. I have seen so fine a climax as that in Jones's *The Hypocrites*—one of the very best in the modern repertory—well nigh ruined by a stock company, when, owing to the purely arbitrary demand that the leading man should have the center at a crucial moment, although in the logic of the action he did not belong there, the two young lovers who were dramatically central in the scene were shunted off to the side, and the leading man, whose true position was in the deep background, delivered his curtain speech close up to the footlights on a spot mathematically exact in its historic significance. True dramatic relations were sacrificed to relative salaries, and, as a result, a scene which naturally receives half a dozen curtain calls, went off with comparative tameness. It was a striking demonstration of the importance of picture on the stage as an externalization of dramatic facts.

If the theater-goer will keep an eye upon this aspect of the drama, he will add much of interest to the content of his pleasure and do justice to a very important and easily overlooked phase of technique. It is common in criticism, often professional, to sneer at the tendency of modern actors, under the stage manager's guidance, continually to shift positions while the dialogue is under way; thus producing an unnecessarily uneasy effect of meaningless action. As a generalization, it may be said that this is done (though at times no doubt, overdone) on a principle that is entirely sound: it expresses the desire for a new picture, a recognition of the law that, in drama, composition to the eye is as truly a principle as it is in painting. And with that consideration goes the additional fact that motion implies emotion; than which there is no surer law in psycho-physics. Abuse of the law, on the stage, is beyond question possible, and frequently met. But a redistribution of the positions of actors on the boards, when not abused, means they have moved under the compulsion of some stress of feeling and then the movement is an external symbol of an internal state of mind. The drama must express the things within by things without, in this way; that is its method. The audience is only properly irritated when a stage moment which, from the nature of its psychology, calls for the static, is injured by an unrelated, fussy, bodily activity. Motion in such a case becomes as foolish as the scene shifting in one of the highest colored and most phantasmagoric of our dreams. The wise stage director will not call for a change of picture unless it represents a psychologic fact.

Two men converse at a table; one communicates to the other, quietly and in conversational tone, a fact of alarming nature. The other leaps to his feet with an exclamation and paces the floor as he talks about it; nothing is more fitting, because nothing is truer to life. The repressive style of acting today, which might try to express this situation purely by facial work, goes too far in abandoning the legitimate tools of the craft. Let me repeat that, despite all the refining upon older, more violent and crudely expressive methods of technique, the stage must, from its very nature, indicate the emotions of human beings by objective, concrete bodily reaction. The Greek word for drama means *doing*. To exhibit feeling is to do something.

Or let us take a more composite group: that which is seen in a drawing room, with various knots of people talking together just before dinner is announced. A shift in the groups, besides effecting the double purpose of pleasing the eye and allowing certain portions of the dialogue to come forward and get the ear of the audience, also incidentally tells the truth: these groups in reality would shift and change more or less by the law of social convenience. The general greetings of such an occasion would call for it. In a word, then, the stage is, among other things, a plastic representation of life, forever making an appeal to the eye. The application of this to the climax shows how vastly important its pictorial side may be.

The climax that is prolonged is always in danger. Lead up to it slowly and surely, secure the effect, and then get away from it instantly by lowering the curtain. Do not fumble with it, or succumb to the insinuating temptation of clinging to what is so effective. The dramatist here is like a fond father loath to say *farewell* to his favorite child. But say the parting word he must, if he would have his offspring prosper and not, like many a father ere this, keep the child with him to its detriment. A second too much, and the whole thing will he imperiled. At the *dénouement*, every syllable must be weighed, nor found wanting; every extraneous word ruthlessly cut out, the feats of fine language so welcome in other forms of literary composition shunned as an arch enemy. Colloquialism, instead of literary speech, even bad grammar where more formal book-speech seems to dampen the fire, must be instinctively sought. And whenever the action itself, backed by the scenery, can convey what is aimed at, silence is best of all; for then, if ever, silence is indeed golden. All this the spectator will quietly note, sitting in his seat of judgment, ready to show his pleasure or displeasure, according to what is done.

A difficulty that blocks the path of every dramatist in proportion as its removal improves his piece, is that of graduating his earlier curtains so that the climax (third act or fourth, as it may) is obviously the outstanding, over-powering effect of the whole play. The curtain of the first act will do well to possess at least some slight heightening of the interest maintained progressively from the opening of the drama; an added crispness perceptible to all who look and listen. And the crisis of the second act must be differentiated from that of the first in that it has a tenser emotional value, while yet it is distinctly below that of the climax, if the obligatory scene is to come later. Sad indeed the result if any curtain effect in appeal and power usurp the royal place of the climactic scene! And this skillful gradation of effects upon a rising scale of interest, while always aimed at, is by no means always secured. This may happen because the dramatist, with much good material in his hands, has believed he could use it prodigally, and been led to overlook the principle of relative values in his art. A third act climax may secure a tremendous sensation by the device of keeping the earlier effects leading up to it comparatively low-keyed and quiet. The tempest may be, in the abstract, only one in a teapot; but a tempest in effect it is, all the same.

Ibsen's plays often illustrate and justify this statement, as do the plays of the younger British school, Barker, Baker, McDonald, Houghton, Hankin. And the reverse is equally true: a really fine climax may be made pale and ineffective by too much of sensational material introduced earlier in the play.

The climax of the drama is also the best place to illustrate the fact that the stage appeal is primarily emotional. If this central scene be not of emotional value, it is safe to say that the play is doomed; or will at the most have a languishing life in special performances and be cherished by the élite. The stage story, we have seen, comes to the auditor warm and vibrant in terms of feeling. The idea which should be there, as we saw, must come by way of the heart, whence, as George Meredith declares, all great thoughts come. Herein lies another privilege and pitfall of the dramatist. Privilege, because teaching by emotion will always be most popular; yet a pitfall, because it sets up a temptation to play upon the unthinking emotions which, once aroused, sweep conviction along to a goal perhaps specious and undesirable. To say that the theater is a place for the exercise of the emotions, is not to say or mean that it is well for it to be a place for the display and influence of the unregulated emotions. Legitimate drama takes an idea of the brain, or an inspiration of the imaginative faculties, and conveys it by the ruddy road of the feelings to the stirred heart of the audience; it should be, and is in its finest examples, the happy union of the head and heart, so blended as best to conserve the purpose of entertainment and popular instruction; popular, for the reason that it is emotional, concrete, vital; and instructive, because it sinks deeper in and stays longer (being more keenly felt) than any mere exercise of the intellect in the world.

The student, whether at home with the book of the play in hand or in his seat at the theater, will scrutinize the skilled effects of climax, seeking principles and understanding more clearly his pleasure therein. In reading Shakespeare, for example, he will see that the obligatory scene of *The Merchant of Venice* is the trial scene and the exact moment when the height is reached and the fall away from it begins, that where Portia tells the Jew to take his pound of flesh without the letting of blood. In modern drama, he will think of the scene in Sudemann's powerful drama, *Magda*, in which Magda's past is revealed to her fine old father as the climax of the action; and in Pinero's strongest piece, *The Second Mrs. Tanqueray*, will put his finger on the scene of the return of Paula's lover as the crucial thing to show. And so with the scene of the cross-examination of the woman in Jones's *Mrs. Dane's Defense*, and the scene in Lord Darlington's rooms in Wilde's *Lady Windermere's Fan*, and the final scene in Shaw's *Candida*, where the playwright throws forward the *scène à faire* to the end, and makes his heroine choose between husband and lover. These, and many like them, will furnish ample food for reflection and prove helpful in clarifying the mind in the essentials of this most important of all the phenomena of play-building.

It is with the climax, as with everything else in art or in life: honesty of purpose is at the bottom of the success that is admirable. Mere effectivism is to be avoided, because it is insincere. In its place must be effectiveness, which is at once sincere and dramatic.

The climax, let it be now assumed, has been successfully brought off. The curtain falls on the familiar and pleasant buzz of conversation which is the sign infallible that the dramatist's dearest ambition has been attained. Could we but listen to the many detached bits of talk that fly about the house, or are heard in the lobby, we might hazard a shrewd guess at the success of the piece. If the talk be favorable, and the immediate reception of the obligatory scene has been hearty, it would appear as if the playwright's troubles were over. But hardly so. Even with his climax a success, he is not quite out of the woods. A task, difficult and hedged in with the possibilities of mistake, awaits him; for the last act is just ahead, and it may diminish, even nullify the favorable impression he has just won by his manipulation of the *scène à faire*. And so, girding himself for the last battle, he enters the arena, where many a good man before him has unexpectedly fallen before the enemy.

Chapter 10

Ending the Play

To one who is watchful in his theater seat, it must have become evident that many plays, which in the main give pleasure and seem successful, have something wrong with the last act. The play-goer may feel this, although he never has analyzed the cause or more than dimly been aware of the artistic problem involved. An effect of anti-climax is produced by it, interest flags or utterly disappears; the final act seems to lag superfluous on the stage, like Johnson's player.

Several reasons combine to make this no uncommon experience. One may have emerged from the discussion of the climax. It is the hard fortune of the last act to follow the great scene and to suffer by contrast; even if the last part of the play be all that such an act should be, there is in the nature of the case a likelihood that the auditor, reacting from his excitement, may find this concluding section of the drama stale, flat and unprofitable. To overcome this disadvantage, to make the last act palatable without giving it so much attraction as to detract from the *scène à faire* and throw the latter out of its due position in the center of interest, offers the playwright a very definite labor and taxes his ingenuity to the utmost. The proof of this is that so many dramas, up to the final act complete successes and excellent examples of sound technique, go to pieces here. I am of the opinion that in no one particular of construction do plays with matter in them and some right of existence come to grief more frequently than in this successful handling of the act which closes the drama. It may even be doubted if the inexperienced dramatist has so much trouble with his climax as with this final problem. If he had no *scène à faire* he would hardly have written a play at all. But this tricky ultimate portion of the drama, seemingly so minor, may prove that which will trip him in the full flush of his victory with the obligatory scene.

At first blush, it would seem as if, with the big scene over, little remained to be done with the play, so far as story is concerned. In a sense this is true. The important elements are resolved; the main characters are defined for good or bad; the obstacles which have combined to make the plot tangle have been removed or proved insurmountable. The play has, with an increasing sense of struggle, grown to its height; it must now fall from that height by a plausible and more gentle descent. If it be a tragedy, the fall spells catastrophe, and is more abrupt and eye-compelling. If comedy be the form, then the unknotting means a happy solution of all difficulties. But in either case, the chief business of this final part of the play would appear to be the rounding out of the fable, the smoothing off of corners, and the production of an artistic effect of finish and finality. If any part of the story be incomplete in plot, it will be in all probability that which has to do with the subplot, if there be one, or with the fates of subsidiary characters. If the playwright, wishing to make his last act of interest, and in order to justify the retention of the audience in the theater for twenty minutes to half an hour more, should leave somewhat of the main story to be cleared up in the last act, he has probably weakened his obligatory scene and made a strategic mistake. And so his instinct is generally right when he prefers to get all possible dramatic satisfaction into the *scène à faire*, even at the expense of what is to follow.

A number of things this act can, however, accomplish. It can, with the chief stress and strain over, exhibit characters in whom the audience has come to have a warm interest in some further pleasant manifestation of their personality, thus offering incidental entertainment. The interest in such stage persons must be very strong to make this a sufficient reason for prolonging a play. Or, if the drama be tragic in its nature, some lighter turn of events, or some brighter display of psychology, may be presented to mitigate pain and soften the awe and terror inspired by the main theme; as, for instance, Shakespeare alleviates the deaths of the lovers in Romeo and Juliet by the reconciliation of the estranged families over their fair young bodies. A better mood for leaving the playhouse is thus created, without any lying about life. The Greeks did this by the use of lyric song at the end of their tragedies; melodrama does it by an often violent wresting of events to smooth out the trouble, as well as by lessening our interest in character as such.

Also, and here is, I believe, its prime function, the last act can show the logical outflow of the situation already laid down and brought to its issue in the preceding acts of the drama. Another danger lurks in this for the technician, as may be shown. It would almost seem that, in view of the largely supererogatory character of this final act, inasmuch as the play seems practically over with the *scène à faire*, it might be best honestly to end the piece with its most exciting, arresting scene and cut out the final half hour altogether.

But there is an artistic reason for keeping it as a feature of good play-making to the end of the years; I have just referred to it. I mean the instinctive desire on the part of the dramatic artist and his cooperative auditors so to handle the cross-section of life which has been exhibited upon the stage as to make the transition from stage scene to real life so gradual, so plausible, as to be pleasant to one's sense of esthetic *vraisemblance*. To see how true this is, watch the effect upon yourself made by a play which rings down the last curtain upon a sensational moment, leaving you dazed and dumb as the lights go up and the orchestra renders its final banality. Somehow, you feel that this sudden, violent change from life fictive and imaginative to the life actual of garish streets, clanging trolleys, tooting motor cars and theater suppers is jarring and wrong. Art, you whisper to yourself, should not be so completely at variance with life; the good artist should find some other better way to dismiss you. The Greeks, as I said, sensitive to this demand, mitigated the terrible happenings of their colossal legendary tragedies by closing with lofty lyric choruses. Turn to the last pages of Sophocles's *OEdipus Tyrannus*, perhaps the most drastic of them all, for an example. I should venture to go so far as to suggest it as possible that in an apparent exception like *Othello*, where the drama closes harshly upon the murder of the ewe lamb of a wife, Shakespeare might have introduced the alleviation of a final scene, had he ever prepared this play, or his plays in general, after the modern method of revision and final form, for the Argus-eyed scrutiny they were to receive in after-time. However, that his instinct in this matter, in general, led him to seek the artistic consolation which removes the spectator from too close and unrelieved proximity to the horrible is beyond cavil. If he do furnish a tragic scene, there goes with it a passage, a strain of music, an unforgettable phrase, which, beauty being its own excuse for being, is as balm to the soul harrowed up by the agony of a protagonist. Horatio, over the body of his dear friend, speaks words so lovely that they seem the one rubric for sorrow since. And, still further removing us from the solemn sadness of the moment, enters Fortinbras, to take over the cares of kingdom and, in so doing, to remind us that beyond the individual fate of Hamlet lies the great outer world of which, after all, he is but a small part; and that the ordered cosmos must go on, though the Ophelias and Hamlets of the world die. The mere horrible, with this alleviation of beauty, becomes a very different thing, the terrible; the terrible is the horrible, plus beauty, and the terrible lifts us to a lofty mood of searching seriousness that has its pleasure, where the horrible repels and dispirits. Thus, the sympathetic recipient gets a certain austere satisfaction, yes, why not call it pleasure, from noble tragedy. But he asks that the last act pour the oil of peace, of beauty and of philosophic vision upon the troubled waters of life.

There is then an artistic justification, if I am right, for the act following the climax, quite aside from the conventional demand for it as a time filler, and its convenience too in the way of binding up loose ends.

As the function of the great scene is to develop and bring to a head the principal things of the play, so that of this final act would seem to be the taking care of the lesser things, to an effect of harmonious artistry. And whenever a playwright, confronting these difficulties and dangers, triumphs over them, whenever your comment is to the effect that, since it all appears to be over, it is hard to see what a last act can offer to justify it, and yet if that act prove interesting, freshly invented, unexpectedly worth while, you will, if you care to do your part in the Triple Alliance made up of actors, playwright and audience, express a sentiment of gratitude, and admiration as well, for the theater artist who has manipulated his material to such good result.

The last act of Thomas's *The Witching Hour* can be studied with much profit with this in mind. It is a masterly example of added interest when the things vital to the story have been taken care of. Another, and very different, example is Louis Parker's charming play, *Rosemary*, where at the climax a middle-aged man parts from the young girl who loves him and whom he loves, because he does not realize she returns the feeling, and, moreover, she is engaged to another, and, from the conventions of age, the match is not desirable. The story is over, surely, and it is a sad ending; nothing can ever change that, unless the dramatist tells some awful lies about life. Had he violently twisted the drama into a "pleasant ending" in the last act he would have given us an example of an outrageous disturbance of key and ruined his piece. What does he do, indeed, what can he do? By a bold stroke of the imagination, he projects the final scene fifty years forward, and shows the man of forty an old man of ninety. He learns, by the finding of the girl's diary, that she loved him; and, as the curtain descends, he thanks God for a beautiful memory. Time has plucked out the sting and left only the flower-like fragrance. This is a fine illustration of an addendum that is congruous. It lifts the play to a higher category. I believe it is true to say that this unusual last act was the work of Mr. Murray Carson, Mr. Parker's collaborator in the play.

One more example may be given, for these illustrations will bring out more clearly a phase of dramatic writing which has not received overmuch attention in criticism. The recent clever comedy, *Years of Discretion*, by the Hattons, conducts the story to a conventional end, when the middle-aged lovers, who have flirted, danced and motored themselves into an engagement and marriage, are on the eve of their wedding tour. If the story be a love story, and it is in essence, it ought to be over. The staid Boston widow has been metamorphosed by gay New York, her maneuvers have resulted in the traditional end; she has got her man. What else can be offered to hold the interest?

And just here is where the authors have been able, passing beyond the conventional limits of story, to introduce, in a lightly touched, pleasing fashion, a bit of philosophy that underlies the drama and gives it an enjoyable fillip at the close. We see the newly wed pair, facing that wedding tour at fifty, and secretly longing to give it up and settle down comfortably at home. They have been playing young during the New York whirl, why not be natural now and enjoy life in the decade to which they belong? So, in the charming garden scene they confess, and agree to grow old gracefully together.

It is excellent comedy and sound psychology; to some, the last act is the best of all. Yet, regarded from the act preceding, it seemed superfluous.

Still another trouble confronts the playwright as he comes at grapples with the final act. He falls under the temptation to make a conventionally desirable conclusion, the "pleasant ending" already animadverted against, which is supposed to be the constant petition of the theater Philistine. Here, it will be observed, the pleasant ending becomes part of the constructive problem. Shall the playwright carry out the story in a way to make it harmonious with what has gone before, both psychologically and in the logic of events? Shall he make the conclusion congruous with the climax, a properly deduced result from the situation therein shown? If he do, his play will be a work of art, tonal in a totality whose respective parts are keyed to this effect. Or shall he, adopting the tag line familiar to us in fairy tales, "and so they lived happily ever after," wrest and distort his material in order to give this supposed-to-be-prayed-for condiment that the grown-up babes in front are crying for? Every dramatist meets this question face to face in his last act, unless his plan has been to throw his most dramatic moment at the play's very end. A large percentage of all dramas weaken or spoil the effect by this handling of the last part of the play. The ending either is ineffective because unbelievable; or unnecessary, because what it shows had better be left to the imagination.

An attractive and deservedly successful drama by Mr. Zangwill, *Merely Mary Ann*, may be cited to illustrate the first mistake. Up to the last act its handling of the relation of the gentleman lodger and the quaint little slavey is pitched in the key of truth and has a Dickens-like sympathy in it which is the main element in its charm. But in the final scene, where Mary Ann has become a fashionable young woman, meets her whilom man friend, and a match results, the improbability is such (to say nothing about the impossibility) as to destroy the previous illusion of reality; the auditor, if intelligent, feels that he has paid too high a price for such a union. I am not arguing that the improbable may not be legitimate on the stage; but only trying to point out that, in this particular case, the key of the play, established in previous acts, is the key of probability; and hence the change is a sin against artistic probity. The key of improbability, as in some excellent farces, *Baby Mine, Seven Days, Seven Keys to Baldpate*, and their kind—where it is basal that we grant certain conditions or happenings not at all likely in life—is quite another matter and not of necessity reprehensible in the least. But *Merely Mary Ann* is too true in its homely fashion to fob us off with lies at the end; we believed it at first and so are shocked at its mendacity.

One of the best melodramas of recent years is Mr. McLellan's *Leah Kleschna*. Its psychology, founded on the assumption that a woman whose higher nature is appealed to, will respond to the appeal, is as sound as it is fine and encouraging. She is a criminal who is caught opening a safe by the French statesman whose house she has entered. His conversation with her is so effective that she breaks with her fellow thieves and starts in on another and better life in a foreign country, where the statesman secures for her honest employment.

It is in the last act that the playwright gets into trouble, and illustrates the second possibility just mentioned; unnecessary information which can readily be filled in by the spectator, without the addition of a superfluous act to show it. The woman has broken with her gang, she is saved; arrangement has been made for her to go to Austria (if my memory locates the land), there to work out her change of heart. Really, there is nothing else to tell. The essential interest of the play lay in the reclaiming of Leah; she is reclaimed! Why not dismiss the audience? But the author, perhaps led astray by the principle of showing things on the stage, even if the things shown lie beyond the limits of the story proper, exhibits the girl in her new quarters, aided and abetted by the scene painter who places behind her a very expensive background of Nature; and then caps his unnecessary work by bringing the statesman on a visit to see how his protégée is getting along. Meanwhile, the knowing spectator murmurs in his seat (let us hope) and kicks against the pricks of convention.

These examples indicate some of the problems centering in an act which for the very reason that it is, or seems, comparatively unimportant, is all the more likely to trip up a dramatist who, buoyed up by his victory in a fine and effective scene of climactic force, comes to the final act in a state of reaction, and forgetful of the fact that pride goeth before a fall—the fall of the curtain! No wonder that, in order to dodge all such difficulties, playwrights sometimes project their climax forward into the last act and so shorten what is left to do thereafter; or, going further, place it at the play's terminal point. But the artistic objections to this have been explained. Some treatment of the falling action after the climax, longer or shorter, is advisable; and the dramatist must sharpen his wits upon this technical demand and make it part of the satisfaction of his art to meet it.

The fundamental business of the last act of a play, let it be repeated, is to show the general results of a situation presented in the crucial scene, in so far as those results are pertinent to a satisfactory grasp of story and idea on the part of the auditor. These results must be in harmony with the beginning, growth and crisis of the story and must either be demanded in advance by the audience, or gladly received as pleasant and helpful, when presented. The citation of such plays as *Rosemary* and *Years of Discretion* raises the interesting question whether a peculiar function of the final act may not lie in not only rounding out the story as such, but in bringing home the underlying idea of the piece to the audience. Surely a rich opportunity, as yet but little utilized, is here. Yet again danger lurks in the opportunity. The last act might take on the nature of a philosophic tag, a preachment not organically related to the preceding parts. This, of course, would be a sad misuse of the chance to give the drama a wider application and finer bloom. But if the playwright have the skill and inventive power to merge the two elements of story and idea in a final act which adds stimulating material while it brings out clearly the underlying theme, then he will have performed a kind of double function of the drama. In the new technique of today and tomorrow this may come to be, more and more, the accepted aim of the resourceful, thoughtful maker of plays.

The intelligent auditor in the playhouse with this aspect of technique before him will be able to assist in his cooperation with worthy plays by noticing particularly if the closing treatment of the material in hand seem germane to the subject; if it avoid anti-climax and keep the key; and if it demonstrates skill in overcoming such obstacles as have been indicated. Such a play-goer will not slight the final act as of only technical importance, but will be alertly on the watch to see if his friend the playwright successfully grapples with the last of the successive problems which arise during the complex and very difficult business of telling a stage story with clearness, effectiveness and charm.

Chapter 11

The Social Significance of the Play

We have now surveyed the chief elements involved in the making of a play and suggested an intelligent attitude on the part of the play-goer toward them. Primarily the aim has been to broaden and sharpen the appreciation of a delightful experience; for the sake of personal culture. But, as was briefly suggested in the chapter on the play as a cultural possibility, there is another reason why the student and theater attendant should realize that the drama in its possibilities is a work of art, and the theater, the place where it is exhibited, can be a temple of art. This other reason looks to the social significance of the playhouse as a great, democratic people's amusement where stories can be heard and seen more effectively, as to influence, than anywhere else or under any other imaginable conditions. It is a place where the great lessons of life can be emotionally received and so sink deep into the consciousness and conscience of folk at large. And so the question of the theater becomes more than the question of private culture, important as that is; being, indeed, a matter of social welfare. This fact is now coming to be recognized in the United States, as it has long been recognized abroad. We see more plainly than we did that when states like France and Germany or the cities of such countries grant subventions to their theaters and make theater directors high officials of the government they do so not only from the conviction that the theater stands for culture (a good thing for any country to possess) but that they feel it to have a direct and vital influence upon the life of the citizens in general, upon the civilization of the day. They assume that the playhouse, along with the school, library, newspaper and church, is one of the five mighty social forces in suggesting ideas to a nation and creating ideals.

The intelligent theater-goer today, as never before, will therefore note with interest the change in the notions concerning this popular amusement that is yet so much more, based upon much that has happened within our time; the coming back of plays into literary significance and acceptance, so that leaders in letters everywhere are likely to be playwrights; the publication of contemporary drama, foreign and domestic, enabling the theater-goer to study the play he is to see or has seen; and the recognition of another aim in conducting this institution than a commercial one looking to private profit: the aim of maintaining a house of art, nourished by all concerned with the pride in and love of art which that implies, for the good of the people. The observer we have in mind and are trying to help a little will be interested in all such experiments as that of the Little Theaters in various cities, in the children's theaters in New York and Washington, in the fast-growing use of the pageant to illuminate local history, in the attempts to establish municipal stock companies, or competent repertory companies by enlightened private munificence. And however successful or unsuccessful the particular ventures may be, he will see that their significance lies in their meaning a new, thoughtful regard for an institution which properly conducted can conserve the general social welfare.

He will find in the growth within a very few years of an organization like the Drama League of America a sign of the times in its testimony to an interest, as wide as the country, and wider, in the development and maintenance of a sound and worthy drama. And he will be willing as lover of fellow-man as well as theater lover to do his share in the movement—it is no hyperbole to call it such—toward socializing the playhouse, so that it may gradually become an enterprise conducted by the people and in the interests of the people, born of their life and cherished by their love. Nor will he be indifferent to the thought that, thus directed and enjoyed, it may in time come to be one of the proudest of national assets, as it has been before in more than one land and period.

And with the general interests of the people in mind, our open-eyed observer will be especially quick to approve any experiment toward bringing the stimulating life of the theater to communities or sections of the city which hitherto have been deprived of amusement that while amusing ministers to the mind and emotions of the hearers in a way to give profit with the pleasure. Catholic in his view, he will just as warmly welcome a people's theater in South Boston or on the East Side in New York, or at Hull House in Chicago, as he will a New Theater in upper New York, or a Fine Arts Theater in Chicago, or a Toy Theater in Boston; believing that since the playhouse is in essence and by the nature of its appeal democratic, it must neglect no class of society in its service. He will prick up his ears and become alert in hearing of the Minnesota experiment, where a rural play, written by a member of the agricultural school, was given under university auspices fifty times in one season, throughout the state. He will rejoice at the action of Dartmouth College in accepting a $100,000 bequest for the erection and conductment of a theater in the college community and serving the interests of both academic and town life. And he will also be glad to note that the Carnegie Institute of Technology, in Pittsburgh, has initiated a School of Drama as an organic part of the educational life. He will see in such things a recognition among educators that the theater should be related to educational life. And, musing happily upon such matters, it will come to him again and again that it is rational to strive for a people's price for a people's entertainment, instead of a price for the best offerings prohibitive to four-fifths of all Americans. And in this fact he will see the explanation for the enormous growth of the moving picture type of amusement, realizing it to be inevitable under present conditions, because a form of entertainment popular in price as well as in nature, and hence populously frequented. And so our theater-goer, who has now so long listened with at least hypothetic patience to exposition and argument, will be willing, indeed, will wish, as part of his watchful canniness with respect to the plays he sees and reads, to judge the playwright, among other things, according to his interpretation of life; and especially the modern social life of his own day and country.

I have already spoken of the need to have an idea in drama; a centralizing opinion about life or a personal reaction to it—something quite distinct from the thesis or propaganda which might change a work of art into a dissertation. Let it now be added that, other things being equal, a play today will represent its time and be vital in proportion as it deals with life in terms of social interest. To put it another way, a drama to reflect our age must be aware of the intense and practically universal tendency to study society as an organism, with the altruistic purpose of seeing justice prevail. The rich are attacked, the poor defended; combinations of business are assailed, and criminals treated as our sick brothers; labor and capital contest on a gigantic scale, and woman looms up as a central and most agitating problem. All this and more, arising from the same interest, offers a vast range of subject-matter to drama and a new spirit in treating it on the stage. Within the last half century the two great changes that have come in human life are the growth in the democratic ideal, with all that it suggests, and the revolutionary conception of what life is under the domination of scientific knowledge. All art forms, including this of the theater, have responded to these twin factors of influence. In art it means sympathy in studying fellow-man and an attempt to tell the truth about him in all artistic depictions. Therefore, in the drama today likely to make the strongest claim on the attention of the intelligent play-goers, we shall get the fullest recognition of this spirit and the frankest use of it as typical of the twentieth century. This is what gives substance, meaning and bite to the plays of Shaw, Galsworthy, and Barker, of Houghton, and Francis and Sowerby, of Moody and Kennedy and Zangwill, at their best. To acknowledge this is not to deny that enjoyable farce, stirring melodrama and romantic extravaganza are not welcome; the sort of play which simply furnishes amusement in terms of good story telling, content to do this and no more. It is, however, to remind the reader that to be most representative of the day the drama must do something beyond this; must mirror the time and probe it too; yes, must, like a wise physician, feel the pulse of man today and diagnose his deepest needs and failings and desires; in a word, must be a social drama, since that is the keynote of the present. It will be found that even in the lighter forms of drama which we accept as typical and satisfactory this social flavor may be detected, giving it body, but not detracting from its pleasurableness. Miss Crother's *Young Wisdom* has the light touch and the framework of farce, yet it deals with a definite aspect of feminism. Mr. Knoblauch's *The Faun* is a romantic fantasia, but is not without its keen social satire. Mr. Sheldon's *The Havoc* seems also farcical in its type; nevertheless it is a serious satiric thrust at certain extreme conceptions of marital relations. And numerous dramas, melodramatic in form and intention, dealing with the darker economic and sociological aspects of our life—the overworked crime play of the day—indefinitely swell the list. And so with many more plays, pleasant or unpleasant, which, while clinging close to the notion of good entertainment, do not refrain from social comment or criticism. The idea that criticism of life in a stage story must of necessity be heavy, dull and polemic is an irritating one, of which the Anglo-Saxon is strangely fond. The French, to mention one other nation, have constantly shown the world that to be intellectually keen and suggestive it is not necessary to be solemn or opaque; in fact, that one is sure to be all the more stimulating because of the light touch and the sense for social adaptability. This view will in time, no doubt, percolate through the somewhat obstinate layers of the Anglo-Saxon mind.

From these considerations it may follow that our theater-goer, while generally receptive and broad-minded in his seat to the particular type of drama the playwright shall offer, will incline to prefer those plays which on the whole seem in some one of various possible ways to express the time; which drama that has survived has always done. He will care most for the home-made play as against the foreign, if equally well made, since its problem is more likely to be his own, or one he can better understand. But he will not turn a cold shoulder to some European drama by a D'Annunzio, a Sudermann, a Maeterlinck or a Tolstoy, if it be a great work of art and deal with life in such universal applications and relations as to make it quite independent of national borders. One of the socializing and civilizing functions of the theater is thus to draw the peoples together into a common bond of interest, a unit in that vast community which signifies the all-embracing experience of being a human creature. Yet the theater-goer will have but a Laodicean regard for plays which present divergent national or technically local conditions of life practically incomprehensible to Americans at large; some of the Gallic discussions of the French ménage, for instance. Terence taught us wisely that nothing human should be alien from our interest; true enough. There is however no good reason why interest should not grow as the matter in hand comes closer to us in time and space. And still more vigorously will he protest against any and all of the wretched attempts to change foreign material for domestic use to be noted when the American producer (or traducer) feels he must remove from such a play the atmospheric color which is of its very life, transferring a rural setting of old England to a similar setting in New England. Short of the drama of open evil teaching, nothing is worse than these absurd and abortive makings over of drama from abroad. The result is neither fish, flesh nor good red herring. They destroy every object of theater enjoyment and culture, lying about life and losing whatever grip upon credence they may have originally possessed. Happily, their day is on the wane. Even theater-goers of the careless kind have little or no use for them.

That the stage of our day, a stage upon which it has been possible to attain success with such dramas as *The Blue Bird, The Servant in the House, The Poor Little Rich Girl, The Witching Hour, Cyrano de Bergerac, Candida, What Every Woman Knows, The Great Divide* and *The Easiest Way* (the enumeration is made to imply the greatest diversity of type) is one of catholic receptivity and some discriminating patronage, should appear to anyone who has taken the trouble to follow the discussion up to this point, and whose theater experience has been fairly large. There is no longer any reason why our drama-going should not be one of the factors which minister to rational pleasure, quicken the sense of art and invite us fruitfully to participate in that free and desirable exchange of ideas which Matthew Arnold declared to be the true aim of civilization. Let us grant readily that the stage story which shows within theater restrictions the life of a land and the outlying life of the world of men has its definite demarcations; that it may not to advantage perform certain services more natural, for example to the church, or the school. It must appeal upon the basis of the bosom interests and passions of mankind and its common denominator is that of the general emotions. Concede that it should not debate a philosophical question with the aim of the thinker, nor a legal question as if the main purpose were to settle a matter of law; nor a religious question with the purposeful finality of the theologian, or the didactic eloquence of the pulpit. But it can and should deal with any question pertinent to men, vital to the broad interests of human beings, in the spirit of the humanities and with the restraints of its particular art. It should be suggestive, arousing, not demonstrative or dogmatic. Its great outstanding advantage lies in its emotional suggestibility. To perform this service, and it is a mighty one, is to have an intelligent theater, a self-respecting theater, a theater that shall purvey rational amusement to the few and the many. And whenever theater-goers, by majority vote, elect it, it will arrive.

It was suggested on an earlier page and may now be still more evident that intelligent theater-going begins long before one goes to the theater. It depends upon preparation of various kinds; upon a sense of the theater as a social institution, and of the renewed literary quality of the drama today; upon a knowledge of the specific problems of the player and playwright, and of the aids to this knowledge furnished by the best dramatic criticism; upon familiarity too with the printed drama, past and present, in a fast multiplying library that deals with the stage and dramatic writing. The last statement may be amplified here.

A few years ago, there was hardly a serious publication either in England or America devoted to the legitimate interests of the stage from the point of view of the patron of the theater, the critic-in-the-seat whom we have so steadily had in mind. Such periodicals as existed were produced rather in the interests of the stage people, actors, producers, and the like. This has now changed very much for the better. Confining the survey to this country, the monthly called *The Theater* has some value in making the reader aware of current activities. The two monthlies, *The American Playwright* and *The Dramatist*, edited respectively by William T. Price and Luther

B. Anthony, are given to the technical consideration of contemporary drama in the light of permanent principles, and are very useful. The quarterly, *The Drama*, edited and published under the auspices of The Drama League of America, is a dignified and earnest attempt to represent the cultural work of all that has to do with the stage; and a feature of it is the regular appearance of a complete play not hitherto in print. Another quarterly, *Poet Lore*, although not given over exclusively to matters dramatic, has been honorably conspicuous for many years for its able critical treatment of the theater and play; and especially for its translations of foreign dramas, much of the best material from abroad being first given English form in its columns. At Madison, Wisconsin, *The Play Book* is a monthly also edited by theater specialists and often containing illuminating articles and reviews. And, of course, in the better class periodicals, monthly and weekly, papers in this field are appearing nowadays with increasing frequency, a testimonial to the general growth of interest. Critics of the drama like W. P. Eaton, Clayton Hamilton, Arthur Ruhl, Norman Hapgood, William Winter, Montrose J. Moses, Channing Pollock, James O'Donnell Bennett, James S. Metcalf, and James Huneker are to be read in the daily press, in periodicals, or in collected book form. Advanced movements abroad are chronicled in *The Mask*, the publication founded by Gordon Craig; and in *Poetry and Drama*. It is reasonable to believe that, with the renewed appreciation of the theater, the work of the dramatic critic as such will be felt to be more and more important and his function will assume its significance in the eyes of the community. A vigorous dramatic period implies worthy criticism to self-reveal it and to establish and maintain right standards. Signs are not wanting that we shall gradually train and make necessary in the United States a class of critic represented in England by William Archer and A. B. Walkley. Among the publishers who have led in the movement to place good drama in permanent form in the hands of readers the firms of Macmillan, Scribner, Mitchell Kennerley, Henry Holt, John W. Luce, Harper and Brothers, B. W. Huebsch and Doubleday, Page & Company have been and are honorably to the fore. In the way of critical books which study the many aspects of the subject, they are now being printed so constantly as plainly to testify to the new attitude and interest. The student of technique can with profit turn to the manuals of William Archer, Brander Matthews, and William T. Price; the studies of Clayton Hamilton, W. P. Eaton, Norman Hapgood, Barrett Clark, and others. For the civic idea applied to the theater, and the development of the pageant, he will read Percy Mackaye. And when it comes to plays themselves, as we have seen, hardly a week goes by without the appearance of some important foreign masterpiece in English, or some important drama of English speech, often in advance of or coincident with stage production. The best work of the day is now readily accessible, where, only a little while ago, book publication of drama (save the standard things of the past) was next to unknown. It is worth knowing that The Drama League of America is publishing, with the cooperation of Doubleday, Page & Company, an attractive series of Drama League Plays, in which good drama of the day, native and foreign, is offered the public at a cost which cuts in two the previous expense. And the Drama League's selective List of essays and books about the theatre, with which is incorporated a complete list of plays printed in English, can be procured for a nominal sum and will give the seeker after light a thorough survey of what is here touched upon in but a few salient particulars.

In short, there is no longer much excuse for pleading ignorance on the ground of inadequate aid, if the desire be to inform oneself upon the drama and matters pertaining to the theater.

The fact that our contemporary body of drama is

making the literary appeal by appearing in book form is of special bearing upon the culture of the theater-goer. Mr. H. A. Jones, the English playwright, has recently declared that he deemed this the factor above all others which should breed an enlightened attitude toward the playhouse. In truth, we can hardly have a self-respecting theater without the publication of the drama therein to be seen. Printed plays mean a claim to literary pretensions. Plays become literature only when they are preserved in print. And, equally important, when the spectator may read the play before seeing it, or, better yet, having enjoyed the play in the playhouse, can study it in a book with this advantage, a process of revaluation and enforcement of effect, he will appreciate a drama in all its possibilities as in no other way. Detached from mob influence, with no confusion of play with players, he can attain that quieter, more comprehensive judgment which, coupled with the instinctive decision in the theater, combines to make a critic of him in the full sense.

For these reasons, the well wisher of the theater welcomes as most helpful and encouraging the now established habit of the prompt printing of current plays. It is no longer a reproach from the view of literature to have your play acted; it may even be that soon it will be a reproach not to have the printed play presented on the boards. The young American man of letters, like his fellow in France, may feel that a literary *début* is not truly made until his drama has been seen and heard, as well as read. While scholars are raking over the past with a fine-tooth comb, and publishing special editions of second and third-rate dramatists of earlier times, it is a good thing that modern plays, whose only demerit may be their contemporaneity, are receiving like honor, and that the dramas of Pinero, Jones, Wilde, Shaw, Galsworthy, Synge, Yeats, Lady Gregory, Zangwill, Dusany, Houghton, Hankin, Hamilton, Sowerby, Gibson, acted British playwrights; and of Gillette, Thomas, Moody, Mackaye, Peabody, Walter, Sheldon, Tarkington, Davis, Patterson,

Middleton, and Kennedy, acted American playwrights (two dozen to stand for two score and more) can be had in print for the asking. It is good testimony that we are really coming to have a living theater and not a mere academic kow-towing to by-gone altars whose sacrificial smoke has dimmed our eyes sometimes to the clear daylight of the Present. Preparation for the use of the theater looks before and after. At home and at school the training can be under way; much happy preliminary reading and reflection introduce it. By making oneself aware of the best that has been thought and said on the subject; by becoming conversant with the history, theory and practice of the playhouse, consciously including this as part of education; and, for good citizenship's sake, by regarding sound theater entertainment as a need and therefore a right of the people; in a word, by taking one's play-going with good sense, trained taste and right feeling, a person finds himself becoming a broader and better human being. He will be quicker in his sympathies, more comprehensive in his outlook, and will react more satisfactorily to life in general. All this may happen, although in turning to the theater his primary purpose may be to seek amusement.

Is it a counsel of perfection to ask for this? Hardly, when so much has already occurred pointing out the better way. The civilized theater has begun to come; the prepotent influence of the audience is recognized. Surely the gain made, and the imperfections that still exist, are stimulants to that further bettering of conditions whose familiar name is Progress.

In all considerations of the theater, it would be a good thing to allow the unfortunate word "elevate" to drop from the vocabulary. It misleads and antagonizes. It is better to say that the view presented in this book is one that wishes to make the playhouse innocently pleasant, rational, and sound as art. If by "elevate" we mean these things, well and good. But there is no reason why to elevate the stage should be to depress the box office—except a lack of understanding between the two. Uniting in the correct view, the two should rise and fall together. In fact, touching audience, actors, playwrights, producers, and the society that is behind them all, intelligent cooperation is the open sesame. With that for a banner cry, mountains may be moved.

Addendum

A hundred years after publication of his book, Richard F. Burton's shrewd analyses of the theater stand up well. Much has changed in the dramatic arts, with short-lived trends in realism, expressionism, impressionism, experimental theater, modernism, surrealism—plus the extension of theater beyond the stage. Burton was present just for the early years of the enormous industry that transformed stage drama captured into film, then talkies, technicolor, animation, into television, video, home theater, 3-D iMax.

Despite these innovations, the art form that is now called "legitimate theater"—actors on a stage with an audience—is as alive now as it was then. As Burton claimed in the very beginning, the immediacy of real people performing just a few feet away from an audience, instantly responding to that night's viewers, is a special experience. First-nighters continue to line up to be first to experience the freshness of a new play.

Surprisingly, a few of the magazines that Burton mentioned a hundred years ago are still going, such as *The Theater*, now retitled *UK Theatre*, originally started in 1894. However, *The American Playwright* and *The Dramatist* both appear to have lasted just a few years in the 19-teens. *The Drama* quarterly lasted to 1922. *Poet Lore* apparently continued publication at least through 1966. *The Play Book* has disappeared. Gordon Craig's *The Mask* continued to 1926. The exceptionally long-lived drama magazines are *Dramatic Publishing* (US, from 1885), the ubiquitous *Playbill* (from 1884), *Variety* (covering all entertainment, but still retains a

"Legit" section, founded in 1905). Britain still has *The Stage Magazine* (1880). Drama for colleges is now covered by *Dramatics Magazine* (since 1929).

Of the authors Burton recommends, a few are still in print: Clayton Hamilton's *The Theory of the Theatre*; Arthur Ruhl, primarily a historian, *Second Nights: People and Ideas of the Theatre Today*; Montrose J. Moses, writing in the 1930s, *Dramas of Modernism and Their Forerunners*, plus several books on the broader sweep of drama from the 18th Century onward. Channing Pollock wrote of theater from a personal perspective. James Huneker concentrates on personalities in theater, music and the arts.

Two theater books are still in print: from the British writer William Archer, *Play-Making: A Manual of Craftsmanship*, which covers the technical aspects of drama. Barrett Clark's *How to Produce Amateur Plays, a Practical Manual* is still used by drama groups. And the Drama League, a support organization, just recently celebrated 100 years of workshops, fellowships, and awards.

Another innovation—Burton also welcomed the new phenomenon of plays appearing in print, in books, thus entering the enduring realm of "literature." Currently, several modern publishers do little else: Samuel French, Dramatic Publishing, Dramatists Play Service, and others, produce books, which are usually produced as softcover stapled booklets.

Richard F. Burton is best-known as an explorer, traveler, and the translator of the prodigious thousand tales of Scheherazade. This book could be seen as a distillation of Burton's broad understanding of the concept of story, in part learned from his massive undertaking of the thousand stories. The paradigm of Scheherazade is that, in order to avoid the fate of death, she would tell a story to the King, but stop short of finishing the tale until the next day. And the next day, she would tell another tale, with the same tactic, and on and on for a thousand days. That intensive schooling in the art of story-telling, which was just part of Burton's lifetime of delving into Asiatic literatures, led him in later life to parsing the elements of drama, specifically in its manifestation in live theater, the most personal art medium of communication. We are fortunate to benefit from his insights, written in an era of maturity for drama—Wilde, Shaw, Ibsen, Rostand—yet before the age of cinema came to dominate entertainment.

Live theater continues to thrive.

—Sasha Newborn, ed.
June 2015

Bandanna Books • Mudborn Press

WRITING
The Art of Writing, Robert Louis Stevenson ISBN 978-0-942208-82-5
How to Tell a Story, Mark Twain ISBN 978-0-942208-81-8
How to Write..., Edgar Allan Poe ISBN 978-0-942208-84-9
Write It Right, Ambrose Bierce ISBN 978-0-942208-83-2
How to See a Play, Richard F. Burton 978-0-930012-70-0

PLAYS
Shakespeare, Romeo and Juliet ISBN 978-0-942208-66-5
Shakespeare, A Midsummer Night's Dream ISBN 978-0-942208-67-2
Shakespeare, Falstaff: Four Plays ISBN 978-0-942208-74-0
James Madison, The Idea of a President ISBN 978-0-942208-61-0
John Milton, (Supplement) Areopagitica ISBN 978-0-942208-38-2
Plato, (Supplement) Apology of Socrates, & Crito ISBN 978-0-942208-39-9

SHAKESPEARE TRANSGENDER PLAYS
Seven Plays with Transgender Characters ISBN 978-0-942208-48-1
As You Like It ISBN 978-0-942208-35-1
Cymbeline ISBN 978-0-942208-55-9
Hamlet, Prince of Denmark ISBN 978-0-942208-59-7
The Merchant of Venice ISBN 978-0-942208-10-8
The Merry Wives of Windsor ISBN 978-0-942208-57-3
The Taming of the Shrew ISBN 978-0-942208-53-5
The Two Gentlemen of Verona ISBN 978-0-942208-56-6
Twelfth Night ISBN 978-0-942208-33-7

SHAKESPEARE DIRECTOR'S PLAYBOOKS
Antony and Cleopatra Director's Playbook ISBN 978-0-942208-76-4
As You Like It Director's Playbook ISBN 978-0-942208-73-3
Hamlet Director's Playbook ISBN 978-0-942208-60-3
Henry V Director's Playbook ISBN 978-0-942208-72-6
Julius Caesar Director's Playbook ISBN 978-0-942208-78-8
King Lear Director's Playbook ISBN 978-0-942208-77-1
Macbeth Director's Playbook ISBN 978-0-942208-36-8
The Merchant of Venice Director's Playbook ISBN 978-0-942208-64-1

A Midsummer Night's Dream Director's Playbook ISBN 978-0-942208-68-9
Much Ado About Nothing Director's Playbook ISBN 978-0-942208-34-4
Othello Director's Playbook ISBN 978-0-942208-46-7
Richard III Director's Playbook ISBN 978-0-942208-71-9
Romeo and Juliet Director's Playbook ISBN 978-0-942208-65-8
The Taming of the Shrew Director's Playbook ISBN 978-0-942208-70-2
Twelfth Night Director's Playbook ISBN 978-0-942208-696

POETRY

Sappho: The Poems ISBN 978-0-942208-11-5
Sappho (Supplement) Poems ISBN 978-0-942208-40-5
Elizabeth Barrett Browning, Aurora Leigh, ISBN 978-0-942208-62-7
Shakespeare, Venus and Adonis ISBN 978-0-942208-75-7
Walt Whitman, Leaves of Grass (1855) ISBN 978-0-942208-08-5
Whitman: Supplement: Leaves of Grass (1855) ISBN 978-0-942208-37-5
Hayashi (Dennis Holt), Tanka Waka Uta ISBN 978-0-930012-67-0
Jorge de Sena , Sobre Esta Praia…, (Portuguese/English) ISBN 978-0-930012-01-4
Paul Portugés, Aztec Birth, (Nahuatl/English) ISBN 978-0-930012-32-8
Astrid Ivask, At the Fallow's Edge, poems (Latvian/English)
Marilyn Coffey, A Cretan Cycle ISBN 978-0-942208-14-6
Dante, Vita Nuova ISBN 978-0-942208-47-4
Dante Gabriel Rossetti, Dante and His Circle ISBN 978-0-942208-09-2
Ossian Legends, James MacPherson. ISBN 978-0-930012-50-2
The Babylonian Captivity, Lesya Ukrainka. ISBN 978-0-930012-52-6
The Deserted Village, Oliver Goldsmith. ISBN 978-0-930012-68-7

FICTION

Harriet Beecher Stowe, Unce Tom's Cabin ISBN 978-0-942208-54-2
Luis Leal, Myths & Legends of Mexico/Mitos y Leyendas de México ISBN 978-0-942208-31-3 (Spanish/English)
Mary Shelley, Frankenstein ISBN 978-0-942208-45-0
Mary Shelley, Matilda ISBN 978-0-942208-49-8
Edgar Allan Poe, The First Detective ISBN 978-0-942208-15-3
Leo Tolstoy, Hadji Murad ISBN 978-0-942208-63-4
Sasha Newborn, The Basement. ISBN 978-0-930012-06-9
The Man Without a Country, Edward Everett Hale. ISBN 978-0-942208-80-1

ANTHOLOGIES
TimeWell monthly litmag: www.timewell.us ISSN 2333-6102
Berlin, The Divided City 1945-1989. (German/English) ISBN 978-0-930012-64-9

LANGUAGE GUIDES
Italian for Opera Lovers ISBN 978-0-942208-17-7
French for Food Lovers ISBN 978-0-930012-61-8
Yiddish, you say? Nu? ISBN978-0-930012-65-6
The Deadword Dictionary ISBN978-0-930012-25-0
Doctorese for the imPatient ISBN978-0-930012-49-6

GENDER
I Ching (he) ISBN 978-0-930012-28-1
I Ching (he/she) ISBN 978-0-930012-30-4
I Ching (he or she) ISBN 978-0-930012-34-2
I Ching (hu) ISBN 978-0-930012-35-9
I Ching (one) ISBN 978-0-930012-37-3
I Ching (s/he) ISBN 978-0-930012-42-7
I Ching (she) ISBN 978-0-930012-44-1
I Ching (they) ISBN 978-0-930012-48-9

www.ingramcontent.com/pod-product-compliance
Lightning Source LLC
Chambersburg PA
CBHW031402040426
42444CB00005B/389